2-495

# BERLITZ®

# ARABIC
## FOR YOUR TRIP

**By the staff of Editions Berlitz**

(US) ISBN 0-02-965150-6
(UK) ISBN 0-304-96515-4

Library of Congress Catalog Card Number: 80-69578

Printed in Great Britain by Fletcher & Son Ltd, Norwich

# Contents

(for complete index, see pp. 190—191)

## Tipping recommendations

The figures below are shown either as a percentage of the bill or in local currency. They indicate a suggested tip for the services described.

In addition, the custom of giving baksheesh is widespread and deeply entrenched in the habits of most Arab countries. Baksheesh is a tip given for any kind of minor service—from taking a picture of an Arab child to having someone show you the way to the spice bazaar. Therefore have plenty of small change on you. Sometimes ballpoint pens or cigarettes may be given instead of coins. And sweets will make you popular with children.

|  | Egypt | Jordan | Lebanon |
|---|---|---|---|
| **HOTEL** | | | |
| Service charge, bill | 17% (incl.) | 10% (incl.) | 12% (incl.) |
| Porter, per bag | 10 piastres | 50–100 fils | £1 |
| Bellboy, errand | 10 piastres | 50 fils | £1 |
| Maid, per week | £1 (optional) | 100 fils | none |
| Doorman, hails cab | 10 piastres | 50–100 fils | 50 piastres |
| **RESTAURANT** | | | |
| Service charge, bill | 10% (incl.) | 10% (incl.) | 10–12% (incl.) |
| Waiter | 5–10% | 5–10% | 5–10% |
| Hat check | 10 piastres | 50–100 fils | 50 piastres |
| Lavatory attendant | 5–10 piastres | 50–100 fils | 50 piastres |
| Taxi driver | 10% and round off | none | none |
| Barber | 25 piastres | 50–100 fils | £1 |
| Women's hairdresser | 25 piastres | 100 fils | 1 £ |
| Theatre usher | 5 piastres | none | none |
| Bootblack (total) | 5 piastres | 50–100 fils | £1 |

# Preface

In response to considerable demand, we have published selected volumes of what has become the world's most popular phrase book series in a hard-cover version. With its larger print and sturdy binding, *Arabic for Your Trip* is ideal for home study prior to departure as well as for use during your journey.

In preparing this book we took into account a wealth of suggestions from phrase book users around the world. The accent is on helping the traveller in practical, every-day situations.

The contents are logically arranged so you can find the right phrase quickly and easily at the moment you need it.

*Arabic for Your Trip* features:

● all the phrases and supplementary vocabulary you'll need on your trip

● complete phonetic transcription throughout, enabling you to pronounce every word correctly

● special panels showing replies your listener might like to give you: just hand him the book and let him point to the appropriate phrase. This is particularly useful in certain difficult situations (trouble with the car, at the doctor's, etc.)

● a wide range of travel facts, hints and useful practical information, providing a valuable insight into life in the Arab world

● a tipping chart (opposite) and a reference section in the back of the book

● the basics of Arabic grammar, enabling you to construct new phrases yourself

Certain sections are particularly appreciated by travellers: the extensive "Eating Out" section which explains what's on the menu, in the soup and under the sauce, with translations, and the complete "Shopping Guide" which enables you to be almost as specific and selective as you would be at home.

Trouble with the car? Turn to the mechanic's manual with its dual-language terms. Feeling ill? Our medical section provides the most rapid communication possible between you and the doctor.

To make the most of *Arabic for Your Trip*, we suggest that you start with the "Guide to Pronunciation". Then go on to "Some Basic Expressions". This not only gives you a minimum vocabulary, it helps you to pronounce the language.

With the Arabic used in this book you can make yourself understood throughout the Middle East. Of course there are considerable differences in vocabularly and usage (see next page). That's why you will sometimes find alternatives for words given in brackets [ ]. If your listener cannot understand the first expression, try the alternative.

We are particularly grateful to Mr. Aly Hussein and Dr. Z. Mahfouz of the Berlitz Schools of Egypt for their help in the preparation of this book, and also to Dr. T. J. A. Bennett for his advice concerning the transcription.

We shall be very pleased to receive any comments, criticisms and suggestions that you think may help us in preparing future editions.

Thank you. And have a good trip.

---

Throughout this book, the symbols illustrated here indicate small sections where phrases have been compiled that your listener might like to say to *you*. If you don't understand him, give him the book and let him point to the phrase in his language. The English translation is just beside.

# A very basic grammar

Classical Arabic is the language of the Koran and dates back to the 7th century. But it has changed through the centuries, and modern spoken Arabic varies greatly from country to country.

This book, destined principally for Egypt, Lebanon and Jordan—but equally useful for the rest of the Middle East—tries to steer a middle course between the spoken and the written (classical) language. When the same (spoken) word is used in all countries, we give that word as the most direct means of communication with the people. But when the word is different from one country to another, we've provided the written (classical) word which is necessarily the same in all countries. Sometimes, however, the classical word is unfamiliar and almost never used. In this case you'll find the Egyptian word with the word(s) used in other countries in brackets [ ].

Arabic is a Semitic language and therefore differs structurally from English and European concepts of language. It is written from right to left.

## Articles

The definite article (the) in Arabic is ال (**æl**) for both the masculine and feminine genders, and the singular and plural. It preceeds the noun and generally the adjective.

| | | |
|---|---|---|
| فندق | **fon**dok | hotel |
| كبير | kæ**bīr** | big |
| الفندق | æl **fon**dok | the hotel |
| الفندق الكبير | æl **fon**dok æl kæ**bīr** | the big hotel |

There is no indefinite article (a/an). To give indefinite meaning the article is simply omitted.

## Nouns

There are two genders, masculine and feminine. In general words ending in **æ** or **a** are feminine. The names of towns and countries are nearly always feminine.

| Masculine | | | Feminine | | |
|---|---|---|---|---|---|
| طالب | tālib | student (m.) | طالبة | tālibæ | student (f.) |
| شارع | shǣri′ | street | وردة | wærdæ | flower |
| دكان | dokkǣn | shop | فرنسا | faransa | France |

There are two sorts of plurals in Arabic: one for two things (double), and another for three or more. Basically, to form the double add the ending ين (**ēn**) to a singular masculine noun, or تين (**tēn**) to a feminine noun. To make the plural for three or more, add the ending ين (**īn**) to singular masculine nouns and ات (**ǣt** or **āt**) to feminine nouns. There are, however, numerous exceptions and irregular plurals where the word changes, like the English "child" to "children". Here are a few examples:

### Regular

| | | | | | |
|---|---|---|---|---|---|
| فنان | fænnǣn | an artist | شجرة | shagara | a tree |
| فنانين | fænnǣnēn | two artists | شجرتين | shagartēn | two trees |
| فنانين | fænnǣnīn | artists | شجرات | shagarāt | trees |

### Irregular

| | | | | | |
|---|---|---|---|---|---|
| ولد | wælæd | a boy | سمكة | sæmækæ | a fish |
| ولدين | wælædēn | two boys | سمكتين | sæmæktēn | two fish |
| أولاد | ′æwlǣd | boys | سمك | sæmæk | fish |

## Adjectives

Adjectives do not come before the noun as in English, but afterwards. They agree with the noun in gender and number. Don't forget that when there is a definite article in front of the noun, the adjective must also be preceeded by the definite article. However, the verb "to be" doesn't exist in the present tense in Arabic. In order to describe something, just put the noun with the definite article, and then the adjective without the article.

| | | |
|---|---|---|
| البيت الكبير | æl bēt æl kæbīr | the big house |
| البيت كبير . | æl bēt kæbīr | The house is big. |

When an adjective qualifies a plural noun that is not human, the adjective is put in the feminine singular.

| | | |
|---|---|---|
| شجرة كبيرة | shagara kæbīræ | a big tree |
| شجرات كبيرة | shagarāt kæbīræ | big trees |

There are no possessive adjectives; instead a suffix is added to the noun. Here are the suffixes for masculine nouns (for feminine nouns insert the letter **t** shown in parentheses):

| | | | | | |
|---|---|---|---|---|---|
| my | ... ي | ...(t)ī | our | ... ن | ...(t)nǣ |
| your(m.) | ... ك | ...(t)æk | | | |
| your(f.) | ... ك | ...(t)ik | your(pl.) | ... كم | ...(t)kom |
| his/its | ... ه | ...(t)oh | | | |
| her/its | ... ها | ...(t)hæ | their | ... هم | ...(t)hom |

Adding a possessive pronoun suffix to a noun makes it definite, and therefore if an adjective follows, the adjective must have the definite article.

| | | |
|---|---|---|
| كتاب كبير | kitǣb kæbīr | a big book |
| كتابى الكبير | kitǣbī æl kæbīr | my big book |

## Verbs

One particularity of Arabic verbs is that they change not only according to the subject (I, you, he, etc.), but also according to whether a man or a woman is spoken to. You'll find examples of this in "Some Basic Expressions" (pages 16–21). In the rest of this phrase book all verbs are given in the masculine form, unless the context shows clearly that you're addressing a woman.

The following is the past and present conjugation of the verb "to write". Note that the subject pronoun is normally omitted.

|  | Present tense | | Past tense | |
|---|---|---|---|---|
| I | أكتب | ′æktob | كتبت | kætæbto |
| you (m.) | تكتب | tæktob | كتبت | kætæbtæ |
| you (f.) | تكتبى | tæktobī | كتبتى | kætæbti |
| he/it | يكتب | yæktob | كتب | kætæbæ |
| she/it | تكتب | tæktob | كتبت | kætæbæt |
| we | نكتب | næktob | كتبنا | kætæbnā |
| you | تكتبوا | tæktobū | كتبتوا | kætæbtū |
| they | يكتبوا | yæktobū | كتبوا | kætæbū |

To form the future tense, add the prefix سـ **(sæ)** to the present tense.

When you want to make a negative sentence, put ما **(mā)** in front of the verb:

| أنا أكتب . | ænā ′æktob | I write. |
|---|---|---|
| أنا ما أكتب . | ænā mā ′æktob | I don't write. |

To ask a question, simply put هل **(hæl)** at the beginning of the sentence:

| البيت كبير . | æl bēt kæbīr | The house is big. |
|---|---|---|
| هل البيت كبير ؟ | hæl æl bēt kæbīr | Is the house big? |

## Personal pronouns

| I | أنا | ænā | | we | نحن | næḥno |
|---|---|---|---|---|---|---|
| you (m.) | أنت | ′intæ | | | | |
| you (f.) | انت | ′inti | | you | أنتم | ′æntom |
| he/it | هو | howæ | | | | |
| she/it | هى | hiyæ | | they | هم | hom |

# Guide to pronunciation

Here are the 28 characters which comprise the Arabic alphabet. A character may have different forms, depending on whether it's used by itself or comes at the end, in the middle or at the beginning of a word.

| Isolated | Final | Median | Initial | Name |
|---|---|---|---|---|
| ا | ا | | | ʼælif |
| ب | ب | ـبـ | بـ | bi |
| ت | ت | ـتـ | تـ | ti |
| ث | ث | ـثـ | ثـ | si |
| ج | ج | ـجـ | جـ | gim |
| ح | ح | ـحـ | حـ | ḥa |
| خ | خ | ـخـ | خـ | kha |
| د | ـد | | | dǣl |
| ذ | ـذ | | | zǣl |
| ر | ـر | | | ri |
| ز | ـز | | | zēn |
| س | ـس | ـسـ | سـ | sin |
| ش | ـش | ـشـ | شـ | shin |
| ص | ـص | ـصـ | صـ | sād |
| ض | ـض | ـضـ | ضـ | da |
| ط | ـط | ـطـ | طـ | ta |
| ظ | ـظ | ـظـ | ظـ | za |
| ع | ـع | ـعـ | عـ | ʼēn |
| غ | ـغ | ـغـ | غـ | gēn |
| ف | ـف | ـفـ | فـ | fi |
| ق | ـق | ـقـ | قـ | kāf |
| ك | ـك | ـكـ | كـ | kǣf |
| ل | ـل | ـلـ | لـ | lǣm |
| م | ـم | ـمـ | مـ | mim |
| ن | ـن | ـنـ | نـ | nūn |
| ة ه | ة ه | ـﻬ | هـ | hi |
| و | و | | | wāw |
| ى | ى | ـيـ | يـ | yi |

This, of course, is not enough to pronounce Arabic. We're offering you a helping hand by providing a transcription throughout this book. This and the following section are intended to make you familiar with our transcription and to help you get used to the sounds of Arabic.

As a minimum vocabulary for your trip, we've selected a number of basic words and phrases under the title "Some Basic Expressions" (pages 16–21).

### An outline of the sounds of Arabic

The traditional Arabic script is composed of consonants only and is written from right to left. A system of vowel signs (small marks above or below the characters), used mainly in the Koran, in poetry and in texts for beginners ensures proper pronunciation.

Written Arabic is fairly uniform. The spoken language, however, can differ considerably from one country to another or even among regions of the same country. We have based our transcription on the dialect used in most parts of Lower Egypt and especially in Cairo. This dialect is widely understood throughout the Middle East thanks to Egyptian films, radio and the recordings of popular artists. In addition, the Egyptian dialect is easier to learn than the others because some difficult sounds have been replaced by simpler ones, so that several letters of the alphabet are pronounced alike.

You'll find the pronunciation of the Arabic letters and sounds explained below, as well as the symbols we use for them in the transcriptions. Of course, the sounds of any two languages are never exactly the same; but if you follow carefully the indications supplied here, you'll have no difficulty in reading our transcriptions in such a way as to make yourself understood.

Letters written **bold** should be stressed (pronounced louder).

## Consonants

| Letter | Approximate pronunciation | Symbol | Example | |
|--------|---------------------------|--------|---------|---|
| ء أ | glottal stop* | ' | أرنب | 'ærnæb |
| ب | like **b** in **b**oy | b | باب | bᾱb |
| ت | like **t** in **t**en | t | تاج | tᾱg |
| ث | in classical Arabic, like **th** in **th**in; in spoken Arabic: | | | |
| | 1) like **s** in **s**it | s | ثورة | sawra |
| | 2) like **t** in **t**en | t | ثور | tōr |
| ج | 1) like **g** in **g**et (Egypt) | g | جميل | gæmīl |
| | 2) like **s** in plea**s**ure (most other countries) | zh | جميل | zhæmīl |
| ح | like **h** in **h**oot, but more "emphatic" and with slight friction in throat | ḥ | حديد | ḥæ**dīd** |
| خ | like **ch** in Scottish lo**ch** | kh | خرج | **kh**aragæ |
| د | like **d** in **d**ay | d | دب | dibb |
| ذ | in classical Arabic, like **th** in **th**en; in spoken Arabic: | | | |
| | 1) like **z** in **z**ebra | z | ذكى | **z**æki |
| | 2) like **d** in **d**ay | d | ذهب | **d**æhæb |
| ر | like **r** in rolled Scottish **r** | r | رجل | **r**ᾱgil |

---

* This corresponds, in English, to the initial blocking of the throat before a vowel, as before the second o in "cooperate". It is also heard in the Cockney pronunciation of t in "water" (wa'er). In Arabic, the glottal stop can occur before a vowel *or* a consonant and even at the end of a word.

| ز | like z in zebra | z | زيت | zēt |
|---|---|---|---|---|
| س | like s in sit | s | سبب | sæbæb |
| ش | like sh in shine | sh | شمس | shæms |
| ص | like s in sun, pronounced with considerable "emphasis" | s | صبر | sabr |
| ض | like d in duck, pronounced with "emphasis" | d | ضيف | dēf |
| ط | like t in tough, pronounced with "emphasis" | t | طيارة | tayyāra |
| ظ | in classical Arabic, like th in then; in spoken Arabic: like z in zebra | z | ظريف | zarīf |
| ع | similar to glottal stop (see above) | ' | رفيع | rafī' |
| غ | like a soft version of ch in Scottish loch (or like French pronunciation of r in "rue") | g | غالى | gāli |
| ف | like f in feed | f | فانوس | fænūs |
| ق | in classical Arabic, an "emphatic" k; in spoken Arabic: 1) like k in kite | k | قلب | kalb |
|  | 2) glottal stop (see above) | ' | قمر | 'amar |
| ك | like k in kite | k | كتاب | kitæb |
| ل | like l in let | l | لطيف | latīf |
| م | like m in meet | m | ملبن | mælbæn |
| ن | like n in neat | n | نرجس | nærgis |
| ﻫ | like h in hear, whatever its position in the word | h | هرم | haram |
| و | like w in well | w | ورد | wærd |
| ى | like y in yell | y | يكتب | yæktob |

## Vowels

The letters ‍ا, و and ى in the list above can also serve as vowels. In addition, Arabic has three vowel signs (´, ', ـ); they occur either above or below the letter and are pronounced after the letter that carries the sign. In contemporary written Arabic—as in this book—the vowel signs are generally omitted. The context shows the reader which is the appropriate vowel he has to supply.

| ´ ا | 1) like **a** in northern English h**a**t or in American wh**a**t (short) | a | صبر | sabr |
| | 2) like **a** in c**a**r (long) | ā | طار | tār |
| | 3) like **a** in c**a**n (short) | æ | كتب | kætæbæ |
| | 4) like **a** in c**a**n, but long | ǣ | كتاب | kitǣb |
| ' و | 1) like **aw** in r**aw**, but with the lips more tightly rounded; it sounds quite reminiscent of **oo** in f**oo**t (short) | o | بن | bonn |
| | 2) like **ou** in f**ou**r (long) | ō | يوم | yōm |
| | 3) like **oo** in b**oo**t (long) | ū | نور | nūr |
| ى | 1) like **i** in s**i**t (short) | i | من | min |
| | 2) like **ee** in m**ee**t (long) | ī | جميل | gæmīl |
| | 3) like **ay** in d**ay**, but a pure vowel, not a diphthong (long) | ē | بيت | bēt |

## Note

1) Each symbol in our transcriptions should be pronounced as shown above, regardless of its position in the word; e.g., **s** always has—even between two vowels or at the end of a word—to be pronounced as in sit, not as in houses.

2) Any consonants written double must be pronounced long; e.g., **kk** should be pronounced like in thi**ck c**oat, **pp** like in lam**p p**ost, **ss** like in ma**ss s**urvey, etc.

# Some basic expressions

| | | |
|---|---|---|
| Yes. | أيوه . | æywæ |
| No. | لا . | læ |
| Please. | من فضلك . * | min fadlak* |
| Thank you. | شكراً . | shokran |
| Thank you very much. | شكراً جزيلاً . | shokran gæzilæn |
| That's all right. | عفواً . | æfwæn |

## Greetings

| | | |
|---|---|---|
| Good morning. | صباح الخير . | sabāḥil khēr |
| Good afternoon. | نهارك سعيد . ** | nahārak sæīd** |
| Good evening. | مساء الخير . | masā'il khēr |
| Good night. | ليلة سعيدة . | lēlæ sæida |
| Good-bye. | مع السلامة . | mæ'æl sælāēmæ |
| See you later. | الى اللقاء . | ilæl lika' |
| This is Mr... | أقدم السيد ... | okaddim assæyid |
| This is Mrs... | أقدم السيدة ... | okaddim issæyidæ |
| This is Miss... | أقدم الآنسة ... | okaddim il āēnisæ |

As pointed out in the grammar section, verbs in Arabic change their endings depending whether the person addressed is a man or a woman. In this section, the phrases said to a **man** are marked with one asterisk (*); those said to a **woman** are marked with two asterisks (**). Phrases not marked do not change.

| I'm very pleased to meet you. | تشَرَّفنا . | tæsharrafna |
| How are you? | كيف حالك ؟ ** | kæyfæ ḥǣlik** |
| Very well, thank you. | بخير . | bikhēr |
| And you? | وأنت ؟ ** | wæ inti** |
| Fine. | كويسة . ** | kwæyyisæ** |
| Excuse me. | آسفة . | 'æsfæ |

## Questions

| Where? | أين ؟ | æynæ |
| Where's...? | أين . . . ؟ | æynæ |
| Where are...? | أين . . . ؟ | æynæ |
| When? | متى ؟ | mætæ |
| What? | ما ؟ | mæ |
| How? | كيف ؟ | kæyfæ |
| How much? | كم ؟ | kæm |
| How many? | كم ؟ | kæm |
| Who? | من ؟ | mæn |
| Why? | لماذا ؟ | limǣzæ |
| Which? | أى . . . ؟ | æyy |
| What do you call this? | ما اسم هذا ؟ | mǣ ism hǣzæ |
| What do you call that? | ما اسم ذاك ؟ | mǣ ism zǣk |
| What does this mean? | ما معنى هذا ؟ | mǣ mæ'nǣ hǣzæ |
| What does that mean? | ما معنى ذاك ؟ | mǣ mæ'nǣ zǣk |

18

## Do you speak...?

| | | |
|---|---|---|
| Do you speak English? | هل تتكلم انجليزى ؟ * | hæl tætækællæm 'ingilīzi* |
| Do you speak German? | هل تتكلمى ألمانى ؟ ** | hæl tætækællæmi 'almāni** |
| Do you speak French? | هل تتكلم فرنسى ؟ * | hæl tætækællæm firinsi* |
| Do you speak Spanish? | هل تتكلمى أسبانى ؟ ** | hæl tætækællæmi 'æspāāni** |
| Do you speak Italian? | هل تتكلم ايطالى ؟ * | hæ tætækællæm 'itāli* |
| Could you please speak more slowly? | من فضلك تكلمى على مهلك . ** | min fadlik tækællæmi 'ælāē mæhlik** |
| Please point to the phrase in the book. | من فضلك أشر الى الجملة فى الكتاب . * | min fadlak æshir ilæl gomlæ fi æl kitāēb* |
| Just a minute. I'll see if I can find it in this book. | لحظة واحدة . سأبحث عنها فى الكتاب . | lahza wāēhidæ sæ'æb hæs 'ænhāē fi æl kitāēb |
| I understand. | أنا أفهم . | ænæ æfhæm |
| I don't understand. | أنا لا أفهم . | ænæ lāē æfhæm |

## Can...?

| | | |
|---|---|---|
| Can I have...? | أريد ... من فضلك ؟ * | orīd...min fadlak* |
| Can we have...? | نريد ... من فضلك ؟ ** | norīd... min fadlik** |
| Can you show me...? | ممكن أن ترينى ... ؟ * | momkin æn torīni |
| Can you tell me...? | ممكن تقوليلى ... ؟ ** | momkin ti'ūlīli** |
| Can you please help me? | ممكن تساعدينى من فضلك ؟ ** | momkin tisāē'idīni min fadlik** |

# Wanting

| I'd like...? | ... أريد | orīd |
|---|---|---|
| We'd like...? | ... نريد | norīd |
| Please give me...? | من فضلك اعطنى . . . ؟ * | min fadlak a'tini* |
| Give it to me, please. | من فضلك اعطيهالى . ** | min fadlik 'aatīhæ li** |
| Please bring me... | من فضلك احضرى لى . . . ** | min fadlik ahdiri li** |
| Bring it to me, please. | من فضلك احضرها لى . * | min fadlak ihdirhæ li* |
| I'm hungry. | أنا جعـانة . | ænæ gæ'ænæ |
| I'm thirsty. | أنا عطشان . | ænæ 'atshān |
| I'm tired. | أنا تعبـانة . | ænæ tææbænæ |
| I'm lost. | أنا تهت . | ænæ toht |
| It's important. | انه مهم . | innæho mohim |
| It's urgent. | انه عاجل . | innæho ægil |
| Hurry up! | بسرعة ! | bisor'æ |

# It is/There is...

| It's... | انه ... | innæho |
|---|---|---|
| Is it...? | هل هو ... ؟ | hæl howæ |
| It isn't... | انه ليس ... | innæho læysæ |
| There's/There are... | يوجد ... | yūgæd |
| Is there/Are there...? | هل يوجد ... ؟ | hæl yūgæd |
| There isn't/There aren't... | لا يوجد ... | læ yūgæd |
| There isn't any/There aren't any. | لا يوجد منه . | læ yūgæd minho |

## A few common words

| | | |
|---|---|---|
| big/small | كبير / صغير | kæbir/saɡir |
| quick/slow | سريع / بطىء | særi'/bati' |
| early/late | مبكر / متأخر | mobækkir/mit'akhkhar |
| cheap/expensive | رخيص / غالى | rakhis/ɡǣli |
| near/far | قريب / بعيد | karib/bæ'īd |
| hot/cold | ساخن / بارد | sǣkhin/bǣrid |
| full/empty | مليان / فاضى | mælyæn/fādi |
| easy/difficult | سهل / صعب | sæhl/sa'b |
| heavy/light | ثقيل / خفيف | ti'il/khæfif |
| open/shut | مفتوح / مقفول | mæftūh/mæ'fūl |
| right/wrong | صحّ / غلط | sahh/ɡalat |
| old/new | قديم / جديد | 'ædim/ɡædid |
| old/young | عجوز / شاب | 'æɡūz/shæb |
| beautiful/ugly | جميل / وحش | ɡæmil/wihish |
| good/bad | حسن / سىء | hæsin/sævyi' |
| better/worse | أحسن / أسوأ | æhsæn/æswæ' |

## A few prepositions and some more useful words

| | | |
|---|---|---|
| at | عند | 'indæ |
| on | على | ælæ |
| in | فى | fi |
| to | الى | 'ilǣ |
| from | من | min |
| inside | داخل | fiddǣkhil |
| outside | خارج | fi æl khǣrig |
| up | فوق | fō' |
| down | تحت | tæht |
| before | قبل | kabl |
| after | بعد | bæ'd |

| with | مع | mæ'æ |
| without | بدون | bidūn |
| through | خلال | khilǣl |
| towards | الى | 'ilǣ |
| until | حتى | ḥættǣ |
| during | أثناء | 'æsnǣ' |
| and | و | wǣ |
| or | أو | æww |
| not | ليس ــ غير | læysǣ gēr |
| nothing | لا شىء | lǣ shæy' |
| none | ولا واحد | wælæ wǣḥid |
| very | ... جداً | ...giddæn |
| also | كمان | kæmæn |
| soon | قريباً | karībæn |
| perhaps | ربما | robbæmæ |
| here | هنا | honæ |
| there | هناك | honǣk |
| now | الآن | æl'ǣn |
| then | بعدين | bæædēn |

# Arrival

You've arrived. Whether you've come by ship or plane, you'll have to go through passport and customs formalities. You'll doubtless have received a customs-declaration form on board. Filling it in before landing will save you time upon arrival. (For car/border control, see page 145.)

There's certain to be somebody around who speaks English. That's why we're making this a brief section.

### Passport control

Your travel agent probably helped you obtain a visa and told you about vaccination requirements for the countries you intend to visit. (Failure to comply with these procedures in advance may cause you unnecessary and time-consuming complications upon arrival in the Middle East.)

| | | |
|---|---|---|
| Here's my passport. | هذا جواز سفرى . | hāēzæ gæwāēz safari |
| I'll be staying... | سأبقى ... | sæ'abka |
| a few days | بضعة أيام | bid'at 'æyyāēm |
| a week | أسبوع | osbū |
| 2 weeks* | أسبوعين | osbū'ēn |
| a month | شهر | shahr |
| I don't know yet. | لا أعرف بعد . | læ aarif bæ'd |
| I'm here on holidays. | أنا هنا فى أجازة . | ænāē honāē fi 'ægāēzæ |
| I'm here on business. | أنا هنا لشغل . | ænāē honāē li shogl |
| I'm just passing through. | أنا مارر من هنا بس . | ænāē māērir min honāē bæss |
| I'm sorry, I don't understand. Is there anyone here who speaks English? | آسف لا أفهم . هل يوجد هنـا أحد يتكلم الانجليزية ؟ | āēsif læ æfhæm. hæl yūgæd honāē æhæd yætækællæm ingilizi |

* see grammar

## Customs

After having your passport stamped by an immigration officer you'll go to customs. The customs officer will either have a quick look at your luggage or just ask what you have in addition to duty-exempt items. The chart below shows what you can bring in duty-free (all allowances are subject to change without notice).

| | Cigarettes | | Cigars | | (grams) Tobacco | Liquor (Spirits) |
|---|---|---|---|---|---|---|
| Egypt | 400 | or | 50 | or | 250 | 1 |
| Jordan | 200 | or | 25 | or | 200 | 1* |
| Lebanon | 500 | or | 25 | or | 200 | 1 |
| * open bottle only; non Jordanians only | | | | | | |

A customs declaration is compulsory in certain Arab countries. You must list all currency, jewellery and mechanical or electrical appliances you're bringing in (cameras, radios, etc.). One copy of this form must be given to the customs officer. You'll keep the other which will be submitted to customs upon your departure. The above items, if personal effects, are duty-free; all the governments want to prevent is their being sold or exchanged by tourists.

| | | |
|---|---|---|
| I've nothing to declare. | ليس عندى شيء أعلن عنه . | læysæ indi shæy' oolin 'ænho |
| I've... | عندى ... | indi |
| a carton of cigarettes | خرطوشة سجاير | khartūshit sægæyir |
| a bottle of whisky | زجاجة وسكى | zogǣgit wiski |
| a bottle of wine | زجاجة نبيذ | zogǣgit nibīt |
| Must I pay on this? | هل يجب أن أدفع عن هذا ؟ | hæl yægib æn' ædfæ æn hǣzæ |

24

| How much? | كم ؟ | kæm |
| It's for my personal use/It's not new. | انها لاستعمالى الشخصى / انها مستعملة . | innæhæ lissti'mæli æshshakhsi/innæhæ mosta'malæ |

| من فضلك افتح هذه الشنطة. | Please open this bag. |
| يجب أن تدفع جمرك عن هذا . | You'll have to pay duty on this. |
| من فضلك ادفع فى المكتب الموجود هناك . | Please pay at the office over there. |
| هل عندك أمتعة أخرى ؟ | Have you any more luggage? |

## Changing money

Travellers aren't allowed to bring Egyptian pounds into Egypt, so don't try to change your money before leaving. You'll have to fill in a form stating how much money you have in cash and traveller's cheques. Keep the copy of this form, for you'll have to present it when you leave, along with each receipt you receive from a bank when you change money during your stay.

You'll be able to change money at a bank at any arrival point.

| I want to change some... | أريد تحويل ... | orīd tæḥwīl |
| traveller's cheques | شيكات سياحية | shikæt siyæḥiyyæ |
| dollars | دولارات | dolarāt |
| pounds | جنيهات | gonæyhæt |
| Where's the nearest bank? | أين أقرب بنك ؟ | æynæ akrab bænk orīd tæḥwīl |
| What's the exchange rate? | ما سعر التحويل ؟ | mæ si'r il tæḥwīl |

FOR BANKS—CURRENCY, see page 134

## Baggage—Porters

| | | |
|---|---|---|
| Porter! | ! [ عتال ] شيال | shæyyæl [ættæl] |
| Can you help me with my luggage? | من فضلك ساعدنى فى حمل الحقائب ! | min fadlak sæ'idni fi ḥaml il ḥaka'ib |
| That's mine. | هذه لى . | hæzihi li |
| The big/small/blue/ brown/plaid one. | الكبيرة / الصغيرة / الزرقاء / البنى / المربعات. | æl kæbira/æl sagira/æl zærkā'/æl bonni/æl morabba'æt |
| There's one piece missing. | ناقص قطعة . | nākis kit'a |
| Take these bags to the... | خذ هذه الحقائب الى ... | khodd hæzihi il ḥakā'ib ilæ |
| taxi | التاكسى | æl tæksi |
| bus | الأوتوبيس | æl 'otobis |
| left-luggage office | الأمانات | æl 'æmænæt |
| How much is that? | بكم هذا ؟ | bikæm hæzæ |
| Get me a taxi, please. | اطلب لى تاكسى من فضلك | otlob li tæksi min fadlak |

*Note:* Porters' rates vary from one country to another. Have some small change ready. (For tipping, see inside back-cover.)

## Directions

| | | |
|---|---|---|
| How do I get to...? | كيف أصل الى ... ؟ | kæyfæ asil ilæ |
| Is there a bus into town? | هل يوجد أوتوبيس للبلد ؟ | hæl yūgæd otobis lil bælæd |
| Where can I get a taxi? | أين أجد تاكسى ؟ | æynæ 'ægid tæksi |
| Where can I rent a car? | أين يمكن تأجير سيارة ؟ | æynæ yomkin tæ'gir sæyyāra |

FOR NUMBERS, see page 175

## Car rental

Car rental agencies operate in most larger centers and rates are usually attractive. You will also be able to hire chauffeur-driven cars through agencies located at most airpots as well as in major cities. It's highly likely that someone at the car-rental agency will speak English, but if nobody does, try one of the following:

| | | |
|---|---|---|
| I'd like to rent... | ... أريد تأجير | orīd tæ'gir |
| a small car | سيارة صغيرة | sæyyāra sagīra |
| a large car | سيارة كبيرة | sæyyāra kæbīra |
| a sports car | سيارة سبور | sæyyāra spōr |
| I'd like it... | ... أريدها | oridohǣ |
| for a day/for 4 days | لمدة يوم / لمدة أربعة أيام | limoddit yōm/limoddit 4 æyyǣm |
| for a week/for 2 weeks | لمدة أسبوع / لمدة أسبوعين | limoddit osbū/limoddit osbu'ēn |
| I'd like to hire a chauffeur-driven car. | أريد تأجير سيارة بسائق . [ رميس ] | orīd tæ'gir sæyyāra bisǣ'ik (ramīs) |
| What's the charge per day? | كم الثمن ليوم ؟ | kæm il tæmæn liyōm |
| What's the charge per week? | كم الثمن لأسبوع ؟ | kæm il tæmæn li 'osbū |
| Does that include mileage? | هل هذا يشمل العداد ؟ | hæl hǣzæ yæshmæl il 'æddād |
| Does that include the services of a chauffeur? | هل هذا يشمل السائق ؟ | hæl hǣzæ yæshmæl il sǣ'ik |
| Is petrol (gasoline) included? | هل هذا يشمل البنزين ؟ | hæl hǣzæ yæshmæl il bænzin |
| Does that include full insurance? | هل هذا يشمل التأمين الشامل ؟ | hæl hǣzæ yæshmæl il tæ'min il shǣmil |
| What's the deposit? | كم التأمين ؟ | kæm il tæ'min |
| I have a credit card. | عندى بطاقة رصيد مصرفى . | indi bitākit rasīd masrafi |

* see grammar

FOR DRIVING LICENCE, see page 145

# Taxi

All taxis have meters, but you might ask the approximate fare beforehand. Taxi drivers expect to be tipped.

In addition to taxis, you'll find a collective-taxi service (sær**vis**) in Lebanon. This is a type of group taxi which follows a fixed route, picking up and letting passengers off along the way. Each pays the same fare and can get on or off anywhere he wishes along the route. This is a very popular means of transportation within cities as well as for inter-urban trips. Collective taxis are cheap, costing scarcely more than the bus.

| | | |
|---|---|---|
| Where can I get a taxi? | أين أجد تاكسى ؟ | æynæ ægid tæksi |
| Get me a taxi, please. | أطلب لى تاكسى من فضلك . | otlob li tæksi min fadlak |
| What's the fare to...? | كم الثمن الى ... ؟ | kæm iltæmæn ilæ |
| How far is it to...? | ما المسافة الى ... ؟ | mæ æl mæsæfæ ilæ |
| Take me to... | خذنى الى ... | khodni ilæ |
| this address/the town centre/the ... hotel | هذا العنوان/ وسط البلد/ فندق ... | hæzæl 'inwæn/wasat il bælæd/fondok |
| Turn left/right at the next corner. | الى الشمال / اليمين فى الشارع القادم . | ilæ æshshimæl/æl yæmin fil shæri' æl kædim |
| Go straight ahead. | استمر الى الامام . | istæmirr ilæl æmæm |
| Stop here, please. | قف هنا من فضلك . | kiff honæ min fadlak |
| I'm in a hurry. | أنا مستعجل . | ænæ mista'gil |
| Could you drive more slowly? | من فضلك سق على مهلك . | min fadlak sūk ælæ mæhlæk |
| Could you help to carry my bags? | من فضلك ساعدنى فى حمل شنطى . | min fadlak sæ'idni fi ḥæml shonati |

# Hotel—Other accommodation

Early reservation (and confirmation) is essential in most major tourist centres during the high season. You may have to pay a supplementary charge on Islamic high holidays.

فندق
(fondok)

Hotel. There's no official classification of hotels in the Middle East, but you'll find those of the highest international standards as well as others which seem to have no standards at all! You'd be well advised to choose a hotel with care, thus avoiding any unpleasant surprise. Your travel agent or the local tourist office usually has a list of hotels in three or more price categories.

بنسيون
(pænsyōn)

Boarding house. Generally occupying a floor of an apartment block, boarding houses are found in most towns. Prices are reasonable, and service is good. If you plan to stay a week or so, ask the manager for a reduction.

شقق مفروشة
(shokæk mæfrūshæ)

Furnished flats (apartments). Found particularly in Cairo and Beirut, such accommodation is cheap and practical for longer stays (several weeks).

بيت شباب
(bēt shæbāb)

Youth hostel. These are found in most Middle Eastern countries. Inquire at the local tourist office or at the Youth Hostels Association in your own country before leaving home.

In this section, we're mainly concerned with the smaller and medium-class hotels. You'll have no language difficulties in the luxury and first-class hotels where most of the staff can speak English.

In the next few pages we consider your basic requirements, step by step, from arrival to departure. You need not read all of it, just turn to the situation that applies.

## Checking in—Reception

| | | |
|---|---|---|
| My name is… | ‫… اسمى‬ | ismi |
| I have a reservation. | ‫. عندى حجز‬ | indi ḥægz |
| We've reserved 2 rooms, a single and a double.* | ‫حجزنا غرفتين . غرفة لشخص وغرفة لشخصين .‬ | ḥægæznæ gorfatēn. gorfa lishakhs wæ gorfa lishakhsēn |
| Here's the confirmation. | ‫هذا تأكيد الحجز .‬ | hǣzæ tæ'kid æl ḥægz |
| I'd like a… | ‫… أريد‬ | orīd |
| single room | ‫غرفة لشخص‬ | gorfa lishakhs |
| double room | ‫غرفة لشخصين‬ | gorfa lishakhsēn |
| suite | ‫جناح‬ | gænǣh |
| room with twin beds | ‫غرفة بسريرين‬ | gorfa bisirirēn |
| room with a bath | ‫غرفة لها حمام‬ | gorfa læhǣ ḥæmmǣm |
| room with a shower | ‫غرفة لها دوش‬ | gorfa læhǣ dosh |
| room with a balcony | ‫غرفة لها بلكونة‬ | gorfa læhǣ bælkōnæ |
| room with a view | ‫غرفة بها منظر جميل‬ | gorfa bihǣ manzar gæmil |
| We'd like a room… | ‫… نريد غرفة‬ | norīd gorfa |
| in the front | ‫فى الأمام‬ | fil æmǣm |
| at the back | ‫فى الخلف‬ | fil khælf |
| facing the sea | ‫تطل على البحر‬ | totill 'ælæl baḥr |
| facing the gardens | ‫تطل على الحديقة‬ | totill 'ælæl ḥædika |

* see grammar

FOR NUMBERS, see page 175

| It must be quiet. | لا بد أن تكون هادئة . | læbodd æn tækūn hædi'æ |
| Is there...? | هل يوجد ... ؟ | hæll yūgæd |
| air conditioning | تكييف هواء | tækyif hæwǣ |
| heating | تدفئة | tædfi'æ |
| a radio/television in the room | راديو / تليفزيون فى الغرفة | radyo/tilivisyōn fil gorfa |
| a laundry | غسيل ومكوة | gæsil wæ mækwæ |
| room service | خدمة فى الغرفة | khidmæ fil gorfa |
| hot water | ماء ساخن | mǣ' sǣkhin |
| running water | ماء جارى | mǣ' gǣri |
| a private toilet | تواليت خاص | twælitt khās |

## How much?

| What's the price...? | كم الثمن ... ؟ | kæm æl tæmæn |
| per night | لمدة يوم | limoddit yōm |
| per week | لمدة أسبوع | limoddit osbū |
| for bed and breakfast | للنوم والفطار | lilnōm wæl fitār |
| excluding meals | بدون وجبات | bidūn wægbǣt |
| for full board | للاقامة الكاملة | lil ikāmæ æl kæmilæ |
| for half board | لنصف الاقامة | linisf æl 'ikāmæ |
| Does that include meals/service? | هل هذا يشمل الوجبات / الخدمة ؟ | hæl hǣzæ yæshmæl æl wægbǣt/æl khidmæ |
| Is there any reduction for children? | هل يوجد تخفيض للاطفال ؟ | hæl yūgæd takhfid lil atfāl |
| Do you charge for the baby? | هل تحاسب على الطفل ؟ | hæl toḥǣsib 'ælæl tifl |
| That's too expensive. | هذا غالى جداً . | hǣzæ gæli giddæn |
| Haven't you anything cheaper? | هل عندك شىء أرخص ؟ | hæl indæk shē' arkhass |

FOR NUMBERS, see page 175

## How long?

| | | |
|---|---|---|
| We'll be staying... | ... سنبقى | sænæbkā |
| overnight only | الليلة فقط | æl lēlæ fakatt |
| a few days | بضعة أيام | bid'at ǣyyǣm |
| a week (at least) | أسبوع ( على الأقل ) | osbū (ælæl akall) |
| I don't know yet. | لا أعرف بعد . | lǣ āraf bæ'd |

## Decision

| | | |
|---|---|---|
| May I see the room? | أريد أن أرى الغرفة من فضلك . | orīd æn aral gorfa min fadlak |
| No, I don't like it. | لا . انها لا تعجبني . | lǣ. innæhǣ lǣ to'gibni |
| It's too... | انها . . . جداً . | innæhǣ...giddæn |
| cold/hot | باردة / ساخنة | bǣridæ/sǣkhinæ |
| dark/small | ضلمة / صغيرة | dalma/sagīræ |
| noisy | دوشه | dæwshæ |
| I asked for a room with a bath. | طلبت غرفة بحمام . | talabt gorfa biḥæmmǣm |
| Have you anything...? | هل عندك شيء ... ؟ | hæl indæk shē' |
| better/bigger | أحسن / أكبر | æḥsæn/akbar |
| cheaper/quieter | أرخص / أهدأ | arkhass/æhdæ' |
| That's fine. I'll take it. | كويس . سآخذها . | kwæyyis. sæ'ǣkhozhæ |

## Bills

Provided an extra room isn't required, there's often a reduction of 50 per cent in luxury and first-class hotels for children up to the age of six, and 30 per cent for 6–12 year-olds. Enquire about a similar arrangement at smaller hotels.

A service charge is normally included in the bill, but you can ask:

| | | |
|---|---|---|
| Is service included? | هل الخدمة محسوبة ؟ | hæl æl khidmæ mæḥsūbæ |

32

## Registration

On arrival at a hotel or boarding house you'll be asked to fill
in a registration form. It asks your name, home address,
passport number and further destination. It's almost certain
to carry an English translation. If it doesn't, ask the desk
clerk:

| | | |
|---|---|---|
| What does this mean? | ؟ ما معنى هذا | mæ mæænæ hǣzæ |

The desk clerk will probably ask you for your passport. He
may want to keep it for a while, even overnight. Don't
worry—you'll get it back. The desk clerk may want to ask
you the following questions:

---

| | |
|---|---|
| أريد أن أرى الباسبور من فضلك . | May I see your passport? |
| من فضلك املأ هذه الاستمارة . | Would you mind filling in this registration form? |
| من فضلك وقِّـع هنا . | Sign here, please. |
| ما طول مدة اقامتك ؟ | How long will you be staying? |

---

| | | |
|---|---|---|
| What's my room number? | ما نمرة غرفتى ؟ | mæ nimrit gorfati |
| Will you have our bags sent up? | من فضلك ارسل العقائب فوق . | min fadlak irsil il hakā'ib fōk |
| I'd like to leave this in your safe. | أريد أن أترك هذا فى الخزنة . | orīd æn ætrok hǣzæ fil khæznæ |

## Service, please

Apart from maids, hotel staff in the Middle East is generally only composed of men.

| | | |
|---|---|---|
| maid | خادمة الغرفة | khǣdimæt æl **gor**fæ |
| manager | المدير | æl **mo**dir |
| room service | الخدمة فى الغرفة | æl **khid**mæ fil **gor**fæ |
| switchboard operator | عامل التليفون | ǣmil il ti**li**fōn |

If you want to call the members of the staff, say: Please (min **fad**lak)!

## General requirements

| | | |
|---|---|---|
| Please ask the maid to come up. | من فضلك اطلب من خادمة الغرفة أن تصعد . | min **fad**lak otlob min khǣdimæt æl **gor**fæ æn tas′ad |
| Who is it? | مين ؟ | min |
| Just a minute. | لحظة واحدة ! | **lah**za wæḥdæ |
| Come in! | أدخل ! | **od**kholl |
| Is there a bath on this floor? | هل يوجد حمام فى هذا الطابق ؟ | hæl **yū**gæd ḥæm**mǣm** fi **hǣ**zæl **tā**bik |
| Please send up... | من فضلك ارسل لنا ... | min **fad**lak irsil læ**nǣ** |
| two coffees/a sandwich | فنجالين قهوة / سندوتش | fingæ**lēn** æhwæ/ sændæ**witsh** |
| a bottle of mineral water | زجاجة مياه معدنية | zo**gǣ**git mi**yǣh** mæ′**dæ**niyyæ |
| Can we have breakfast in our room? | هل يمكن الافطار فى غرفتنا؟ | hæl **yom**kin æl ′**if**tār fi gorfati**nǣ** |
| May I have a/an/some...? | من فضلك أريد ... | min **fad**lak o**rid** |
| ashtray | طفاية سجاير | taf**fā**yit sæ**gǣ**yir |
| bath towel | فوطة حمام | **fū**tit ḥæm**mǣm** |

| English | Arabic | Transliteration |
|---|---|---|
| extra blanket | بطانية زيادة | battaniyya ziyǣdæ |
| envelopes | ظروف | zorūf |
| (more) hangers | علاقات ( زيادة ) | ællǣkāt (ziyǣdæ) |
| hot-water bottle | قربة ماء ساخن | irbit mǣ' sǣkhin |
| ice cubes | قطع ثلج | kita' tælg |
| needle and thread | ابرة وخيط | ibræ wæ khēt |
| extra pillow | مخدة زيادة | mækhæddæ ziyǣdæ |
| reading-lamp | لمبة للقراءة | lamba lil kirā'a |
| soap | صابون | sabūn |
| writing-paper | ورق للكتابة | wæræ' lil kitǣbæ |
| Where's the...? | أين يوجد ... ؟ | æynæ yūgæd |
| bar | البار | æl bār |
| barber's | حلاق | ḥællāk |
| bathroom | الحمام | æl ḥæmmǣm |
| beauty salon | صالون التجميل | salōn æl tægmil |
| dining room | صالة الطعام | sālit æl ta'ām |
| restaurant | المطعم | æl mat'am |
| television room | صالة التليفزيون | sālit æl tilivisyōn |
| toilet | التواليت | æl twælitt |

## Breakfast

In the Middle East, breakfast consists of *fool* (black beans), white cheese, *halava* (a sugary confection) and *falafel* (fried balls of ground *fool*). If this doesn't suit your palate, most top-class hotels serve continental or American breakfasts.

| | | |
|---|---|---|
| I'll have a/an/some... | أريد ... | orīd |
| eggs | بيض | bēd |
| boiled egg | بيضة مسلوقة | bēda mæslu'æ |
| soft/medium/hard | نصف سواء/متوسط/جـامد | nisf siwæ/motæwassit/gǣmid |
| fried egg | بيضة مقلية | bēda makliyya |

| | | |
|---|---|---|
| fruit juice | عصير فاكهة | assīr fǣkihæ |
| grapefruit/orange | جريب فروت/برتقال | grēp frūt/bortokāl |
| pineapple/tomato | أناناس/طماطم | ænænǣs/tamātim |
| omelet | عجة | 'igga |
| May I have some...? | أريد ... من فضلك | orīd...min fadlak |
| bread/toast | خبز / توست | khobz/tost |
| hot/cold milk | لبن ساخن / لبن بارد | læbæn sǣkhin/ læbæn bǣrid |
| cream/sugar | كريم / سكر | krēm/sokkar |
| more butter | زبد زيادة | zibdæ ziyǣdæ |
| salt/pepper | ملح / فلفل | mælḥ/filfil |
| coffee/tea | قهوة / شاى | æhwæ/shǣy |
| hot chocolate | شكولاتة ساخنة | shokolāta sokhnæ |
| lemon/honey | ليمون / عسل | læmūn/æsæl |
| jam/marmalade | مربى / مربى برتقال | marabba/marabbit bortokāl |
| Could you bring me a... | من فضلك احضرلى ... | min fadlak iḥdir li |
| plate | صحن | sahn |
| glass | كباية | kobbǣyæ |
| cup | فنجان | fingǣn |
| knife | سكينة | sikkīnæ |
| fork | شوكة | shōkæ |
| spoon | ملعقة | mil'aka |

## Difficulties

| | | |
|---|---|---|
| The ... doesn't work. | ال ... لا يعمل . | il...lǣ yæ'mæl |
| air conditioner | تكييف الهواء | tækyīf hæwǣ |
| fan | مروحة | marwaḥa |
| light | نور | nūr |
| tap | صنبور [حنفية] | sonbūr [ḥænæfiyyæ] |
| toilet | تواليت | twælitt |

FOR EATING OUT, see pages 38–64

| The wash basin is blocked. | . الحوض مسدود | æl ḥōd mæsdūd |
| The window is jammed. | الشباك من الصعب فتحه. | æl shibbǣk min æl saab fætho |
| The blind is stuck. | . الغمامات لا تعمل | æl gæmæmǣt læ tææmæl |
| These aren't my shoes. | . هذا ليس حذائى | hǣzæ læysæ ḥizǣ'i |
| This isn't my laundry. | . هذا ليس غسيلى | hǣzæ læysæ gæsīli |
| There's no hot water. | . لا يوجد ماء ساخن | læ yūgæd mǣ' sǣkhin |
| I've lost my watch. | . ساعتى ضاعت | sǣ'æti dā'it |
| I've left my key in my room. | لقد تركت المفتاح فى غرفتى . | tarakt æl moftǣḥ fi gorfati |
| The bulb is burnt out. | . لمبة النور محروقة | lambit æl nūr mæḥrūka |
| The ... is broken. | . ال ... مكسور | æl ... maksūr |
| lamp | مصباح | misbāḥ |
| plug | كبس | kobs |
| shutter/window shade | شيش / غمامات | shish/gæmmæmǣt |
| switch | مفتاح النور | moftǣḥ æl nūr |
| Can you get it fixed? | هل يمكن اصلاحها ؟ | hæl yomkin islāḥihǣ |

## Telephone—Mail—Callers

| Can you get me Cairo 1 2 3 4 5 6 ? | أريد الاتصال بالقاهرة رقم ١٢٣٤٥٦ . | orīd æl 'ittisāl bil kāhira rakam 12 34 56 |
| Did anyone telephone me? | هل اتصل بى أحد تليفونياً؟ | hæl ittasala bi 'æḥæd tilifōniyyæn |
| Is there any mail for me? | هل توجد خطابات لى؟ | hæl tūgæd khitabǣt li |
| Have you any stamps? | هل عندك طوابع بريد ؟ | hæl ændæk tawābi' bærīd |
| Would you please mail this for me? | هل يمكنك ارسال هذا بالبريد ؟ | hæl yomkinæk irsæl hǣza bil bærīd |
| Are there any messages for me? | هل توجد رسالة لى؟ | hæl tūgæd risǣlæ li |

FOR POST OFFICE AND TELEPHONE, see page 137

# Checking out

| May I have my bill, please? Room 398. | أريد فاتورة حسابى من فضلك غرفة رقم ٣٩٨ . | orīd fatūrit ḥisāebi min fadlak. gorfæ rakam 398 |
|---|---|---|
| I'm leaving early tomorrow. | سأرحل مبكراً صباح الغد . | sæ'arḥal mobækkiran sabāḥ æl gædd |
| Please have my bill ready. | من فضلك جهز لى الفاتورة. | min fadlak gæhhizli æl fatūra |
| We'll be checking out around noon. | سنرحل حوالى الظهر . | sænarḥal ḥawæli æl zohr |
| I must leave at once. | لا بد أن أرحل فوراً . | læbodd æn arḥal fawran |
| Does this include service? | هل هذا يشمل الخدمة ؟ | hæl hæēzæ yæshmæl æl khidmæ |
| Is everything included? | هل كل شىء محسوب ؟ | hæl koll shē' mæḥsūb |
| You've made a mistake in this bill, I think. | أظن أنك أخطأت فى حساب هذه الفاتورة . | azonn 'ænnækæ akhta't fi ḥisæēb hæēzihi æl fatūra |
| Can you get us a taxi? | من فضلك اطلب لنا تاكسى . | min fadlak otlob lænæē tæksi |
| When's the next... to Cairo? | متى موعد ... القادم الى القاهرة ؟ | mætæ maw'id æl..æl kādim ilæē ælkāhira |
| bus/train/plane | الأوتوبيس / القطار / الطائرة | æl 'otobīs/æl kitār/ æl tā'ira |
| Would you send someone to bring down our baggage? | من فضلك ارسل أحداً لانزال الحقائب . | min fadlak irsil 'æḥædæn li'inzæl æl ḥakā'ib |
| We're in a great hurry. | اننا فى غاية الاستعجال . | innænæē fi gāyæt æl 'isti'gæēl |
| Here's the forwarding address. You have my home address. | هذا هو عنواننا القادم . عندك عنوان منزلى . | hæēzæ howæ inwænonæē æl kādim. indæk innwæēn mænzili |
| It's been a very enjoyable stay | كانت الاقامة ممتعة جداً . | kænæt æl 'ikāma momti'æ giddæn |

FOR TAXI, see page 27

# Eating out

There are many types of places where you can eat and drink in the Arab countries.

مطعم
(mat'am)
A restaurant; there's often a set menu, especially in European ones.

حــاتى
(ḥāti)
A restaurant specializing in charcoal-grilled lamb.

مطعم لحم مشوى
(mat'am laḥm mæshwi)
Same as the above, only the name is different in Lebanon.

مطعم حمــام
(mat'am ḥæmāem)
A restaurant specializing in pigeon or squab

مطعم سمك
(mat'am sæmæk)
Fish and seafood restaurant.

فول وفــلافل
(fūl wæ fælāefil)
A snack-bar; this is a popular type of eating place serving *fool* (black-bean dish) and *falafel* (small balls of ground black beans, fried and served with a choice of spices). *Fool* and *falafel* may also be a filling for sandwiches.

كافيتريــا
(kæfitiryæ)
A snack-bar; you may have to eat standing up.

محــل عصير
(mæḥæl 'asīr)
Fruit-juice bar (sometimes it's a drive-in); features fresh fruit juice. Often you can get *shawerma*—thin slices of spitroasted lamb—and sandwiches.

صالون شاى
(salōn shāey)
A coffee shop; it's often a part of a pastry shop.

حلويــات شامى
(ḥælæwiyyāet shāemi)
A Lebanese or Syrian pastry shop.

ملهى ليــلى
(mælhāe læyli)
Night-club (cabaret); dinner and a show; in Egypt all the shows feature the famed belly dancers whom you won't want to miss.

**كاس عرق ومــازة**
(kāēs 'arak wæ māēzæ) A restaurant in Lebanon which serves salads
and appetizers among other local dishes.
This type of restaurant traditionally serves
*arak,* an aniseed liqueur and the national
drink, as beverage.

There are also neighbourhood restaurants, many of which
specialize in a particular dish such as *kosharee* (rice, lentils
and hot sauce), *kebda wa mokh* (liver and brains) or *fiseekh*
(dried fish).

## Eating habits

In this section we're primarily concerned with restaurants—and with lunch and dinner. We assume that you've
already had breakfast at your hotel.

In the Arab countries, meals are generally eaten later than at
home—both privately and in restaurants.

**غـذاء**
(gæedæ) Lunch is generally served from 1 to 3 p.m.

**عشــاء**
('æshæ) Dinner is served from 8 to 11 p.m. In night-clubs you'll be
able to dine even after midnight.

If you feel hungry at an unusual hour, you'll always be able
to find a restaurant or a snack-bar serving warm dishes or
snacks at any time of the day or night.

Most large restaurants in major cities specialize in European
dishes, especially French and Italian, rather than Middle
Eastern cuisine. But you'll usually find some Middle Eastern
dishes on the menu. Unless you're specifically looking for
European food, avoid the big restaurants and go to local
eating places.

In summer many restaurants as well as night-clubs move
outdoors to take advantage of the fine weather.

FOR BREAKFAST, see page 34

## What is Ramadan?

The month of Ramadan is one of Islam's holy periods. As it's a lunar month, it has no regular corresponding date in the calendar year. It's observed by Moslems in all Arab countries by fasting and by refraining from drinking and smoking from sunrise to sunset. This religious rite is a way of showing one's obedience to God and of strengthening social relations.

The main meal of the day which is taken at sunset is called *iftar*. It usually starts with a hot soup, then goes on with *fool* and eggs, generally mixed together, and the rest of the meal is a normal one, followed by oriental sweets. The characteristic drink of this month (non-alcoholic, of course) is *kamar-eldin*. It's made of a stewed apricot purée which is served fresh. Just try it and you'll surely ask for more.

*Iftar* provides the opportunity to meet friends and relatives; it's also a time of charity when beggars, who knock at the door at this special period of the year, will be given food. After *iftar*, people usually listen to music and to readings from the Koran on the radio and go to the mosque. Restaurants and cafés stay open all night and are well patronized.

Later on, at about 1 or 2 a.m., you take your second meal of the "day", called *sohur*, which helps the Moslem to endure the long hours of fasting to come.

During Ramadan, public places are open all night and the streets are brightly illuminated. Nevertheless, one shouldn't forget that the month of Ramadan is first and foremost a religious month.

But don't worry: non-Moslem visitors aren't expected to fast. You'll find eating places open specially for you.

## Hungry

| I'm hungry/I'm thirsty. | . أنا جوعان / أنا عطشان | 'ænæ gæ'ǣn/'ænǣ 'atshān |
| Can you recommend a good (and inexpensive) restaurant? | من فضلك انصحنى بمطعم جيد (ورخيص) . | min fadlak 'insaḥni bimat'am gæyyid (wæ rakhīs) |
| I'd like to reserve a table for 4. | أريـد أن أحجز ترابيـزة ﴾ طاولة ﴿ لـ ٤ . | orīd æn 'æḥgiz tarabēza [tawla] li 4 |
| We'll come at 8. | . سنأتى الساعة ٨ | sænæ'ti æl sǣæ 8 |

## Asking and ordering

| Could we have a...? | ... من فضلك نـريد | min fadlak norīd |
| table in the corner | ترابيزة ﴾ طاولة ﴿ منعزلة | tarabēza [tawla] mon'æzilæ |
| table by the window | ترابيزة ﴾ طاولة ﴿ بجانب الشباك | tarabēza [tawla] bigǣnib æl shibbǣk |
| table outside | ترابيزة ﴾ طاولة ﴿ فى الخـارج | tarabēza [tawla] fil khǣrig |
| What's the price of the set menu? | ما هو ثمن الوجبة ؟ | mǣ howæ tæmæn æl wægbæ |
| Is service included? | هل الخدمة محسوبة ؟ | hæl æl khidmæ mæḥsūbæ |
| Could we have a(n) ... please? | ... من فضلك نـريد | min fadlak norīd |
| ashtray | طفاية سجاير ﴾ منفضة ﴿ | taffāyit sægǣyir [manfada] |
| finger bowl | كاس ماء لغسل الأصابع | kǣs mayya ligæsl æl'asābi' |
| fork | شوكـة | shōkæ |
| glass | كبـاية | kobbǣyæ |
| knife | سكينـة | sikkīnæ |
| plate | صحن | saḥn |
| serviette (napkin) | فوطـة | fūta |
| spoon | ملعقـة | mal'aka |
| tablecloth | مفرش سفرة | mafrash sofra |
| toothpick | مسلكـة أسنان | mæslækit 'æsnǣn |

FOR COMPLAINTS, see page 59

| | | |
|---|---|---|
| I'd like a/an/some... | ... أريـــد | orīd |
| beer | بيـــرة | bīræ |
| bread | عيش [ خبز ] | 'ēsh [khobz] |
| butter | زبـــدة | zibdæ |
| cheese | جبنــة | gibnæ |
| chips (french fries) | شيــبس | ships |
| coffee | قهـــوة | 'æhwæ |
| fish | سمــك | sæmæk |
| fowl | دجـــاج | dægāēg |
| fruit | فاكهــة | fækhæ |
| ice-cream | جلاس [ بوظة ] | glāēs [būza] |
| lemon | ليمون [ حامض ] | læymūn [ḥāmid] |
| lettuce | خس | khass |
| meat | لحم | læḥm |
| milk | لبن حليب | læbæn ḥælib |
| mineral water | ميـاه معدنية | mayya mæ'dæniyyæ |
| mustard | مستردة [ خردل ] | mostarda [khærdæl] |
| noodles | مكرونة شريط | makarōna shirīt |
| olive oil | زيت زيتـون | zēt zætūn |
| pepper | فلفـــل [ بهار ] | filfil [bohār] |
| potatoes | بطاطس | batātis |
| rice | رز | roz |
| rolls | خبز سندوتش | khobz sændæwitsh |
| salad | صلطــة | salata |
| salt | ملح | mælḥ |
| sandwich | سنــدوتش | sændæwitsh |
| soup | شوربــة | shorba |
| sugar | سكــر | sokkar |
| tea | شـــاى | shāēy |
| vegetables | خضـــار | khodār |
| vinegar | خــل | khæl |
| (iced) water | ميـاه ( مثلجة ) | mayya (mitælligæ) |
| wine | نبــيذ | nibīt |

## What's on the menu

Our menu is presented according to courses. Under each heading you'll find an alphabetical list of dishes in Arabic with their English equivalents. This list—which includes everyday and special dishes—will enable you to make the most of an Arabic menu.

Here's our guide to good eating and drinking. Turn to the course you want to start with.

Arab cooking is in many ways typical of what you'll find throughout the Mediterranean. Many popular dishes of Egypt, for example, have been inherited from the Turks or the Circassians, a Moslem people who emigrated from Russia in the last century. Much emphasis is placed on grilling or slowly braising vegetable or meat stews.

## Appetizers—Starters

It's customary in Arab countries to serve a variety of appetizers and salads with the aperitif. These are called the *mezza*. This consists of numerous small plates of hors d'œuvre. Lebanon is especially noted for the diversity and tastiness of its *mezza*. A complete one consists of about 40 different appetizers. We don't have room to name them all, but here's a sampling of some popular ones.

| | | | |
|---|---|---|---|
| I'd like an appetizer. | أريد فاتح شهية من فضلك . | orīd fǣtiḥ shæhiyyæ min fadlak | |
| أنشوجـــة | | 'ænshūgæ | anchovies |
| اسبرجس | | 'asparagas | asparagus tips |
| خرشوف [ أرضى شوكى ] | | kharshūf ['ardi shōki] | artichokes |
| بيـــض | | bēd | eggs |
| بيض بالمايونيز | | bēd bil mæyonēz | egg salad |
| رنجـة | | ringæ | herring |
| رنجـة مملحة | | ringæ momællæḥæ | salted-herring fillets |
| زيتـون | | zætūn | olives |
| مغللات [ كبيس ] | | mikhællilǣt [kæbīs] | pickles (pickled vegetables) |
| كبـد الوز | | kæbid ælwiz | goose-liver pâté |
| كبـد دجاج | | kæbid dægǣg | chopped chicken liver |
| عصير فاكهـة | | 'asīr fækhæ | fruit juice |
| شمـام | | shæmmǣm | melon |
| سـلامى | | sælǣmi | salami |
| سجق [ مقـانق ] | | sogo' [mæ'ǣnik] | sausages |
| سردين | | særdīn | sardines |
| كركنـد | | karakænd | lobster |
| باتيـه [ فواجرا ] | | pǣtēh [fwagrā] | pâté |
| جندفلى [ محـار ] | | gændofli [maḥḥār] | oysters |
| كافيـار | | kavyār | caviar |

## Arabic specialities

باذنجان مغلـــل
(bitingǣn mikhællil)

aubergine (eggplant) stuffed with herbs, garlic and spices.

ورق عنب محشي
(wæræ' 'inæb mæhshi)

grape leaves stuffed with rice and minced meat; may be served cold or hot.

طحينـــة
(tihina)

a paste made with ground sesame seeds and spices; particularly good with fish.

بابا غنوج
(babagænnūg)

*tehina* to which mashed aubergine (eggplant) is added.

حمص بطحينـــة
(hommos bithina)

a spicy paste made with ground chick-peas, *tehina* and spices.

جبنة بيضاء بالطماطم
(gibnæ bēda bil tamātim)

white cheese served with tomatoes, onion, parsley, oil and lemon; sometimes a hot sauce is added.

بطــارخ
(batārikh)

"Egyptian caviar", red fish roe

عجـــة
('iggæ)

omelet, made of onions, parsley and green pepper; baked.

## Salads

What salads do you have?

ما أصناف الصلاطة عندكم ؟

mæ 'asnāf ælsalata ændokom

| | | |
|---|---|---|
| صلاطة خيـار وطماطم [بندورة] | salatit khiyār wæ tamā-tim [banadūra] | cucumber and tomato salad |
| صلاطة بطاطس | salatit batātis | potato salad |
| صلاطـة كرفس | salatit karafs | celery salad |
| صلاطـة خس | salatit khass | lettuce salad |
| صلاطة باذنجان | salatit bitingǣn | aubergine (eggplant) salad |
| صلاطة بنجر [شمندر] | salatit bangar | beetroot salad |
| صلاطـة جرجير | salatit gærgīr | watercress salad |

46

## Salad specialities

Can you recommend a local speciality?

من فضلك انصحني بأكلة محلية .

min fadlak 'insaḥni bi 'æklæ mæḥælliyyæ

لبن زبادي وخيــار
(læbæn zæbǣdi wæ khiyār)

diced cucumbers with a dressing of yogurt, olive oil, garlic and mint leaves

صلاطة بلــدى
(salata bælædi)

salad of cucumbers, tomatoes, onions, watercress, parsley, green peppers, mint leaves (Egypt)

تبولــة
(tæbbūlæ)

Lebanese salad, similar to the Egyptian one, but with cracked wheat and bread crumbs

## Cheese

In Arab countries a lot of cheese is eaten, and it's eaten with the meal, not after the main course. Moreover, it's served most frequently with breakfast and supper. You'll also find it served under various guises as a part of the *mezza*, or appetizers.

جبنة بيضاء من لبن معيز
(gibnæ bēda min læbæn mi'īz)

white goat's milk cheese

جبنة مالحــة
(gibnæ mælḥæ)

salted fresh-curd cheese

جبنــة أريش
(gibnæ 'ærish)

full, rich cheese, slightly salty

جبنة ريكوتــا
(gibnæ rikotta)

a type of cottage cheese

مش
(mesh)

well aged, very salty and sharp

لبنــة
(læbnæ)

a fresh-curd cheese sprinkled with olive oil

## Soup

You'll find many different kinds of soup in the Middle East, among them many European and American favourites as well as regional specialities. Lentil soup is the most popular of the local soups.

| | | |
|---|---|---|
| I'd like some soup. | أريد شوربة من فضلك . | orīd shorba min fadlak |
| What do you recommend? | بم تنصح ؟ | bimæ tansaḥ |

| | | |
|---|---|---|
| شوربة عدس | shorbit 'æds | lentil soup |
| شوربة فراخ [دجاج] | shorbit firǣkh | chicken soup |
| شوربة لحم | shorbit læḥm | meat soup |
| شوربة باذلاء | shorbit bisillæ | pea soup |
| شوربة خضار | shorbit khodār | vegetable soup |
| شوربة سمك | shorbit sæmæk | fish soup |
| شوربة بصل | shorbit basal | onion soup |
| شوربة طماطم [بندورة] | shorbit tamātim [banadūra] | tomato soup |
| شوربة شعرية | shorbit shi'riyyæ | noodle soup |
| شوربة عدس بحامض | shorbit 'æds biḥāmid | lentil and lemon soup (Lebanon) |

## Fish and seafood

Alexandria and Beirut are especially good places to sample fish and seafood, and you'll want to try the grilled shrimps. Aboukir is a fishing village near Alexandria where you can taste the catch fresh from the Mediterranean. If you're lucky, a fisherman may suggest grilling a fish for you right at the seaside. In Cairo, you're likely to eat fish from the Nile. Very often you'll find there is a fishmonger's attached to the restaurant. Consequently you can be sure of having fresh fish and can even pick the one you want for dinner.

| | | |
|---|---|---|
| I'd like some fish. | . أريد سمكاً من فضلك | orīd sæmæk min fadlak |
| What kinds of seafood do you have? | أى أصناف السمك عندكم ؟ | 'æyy 'asnāf æl sæmæk 'ændokom |

In addition to a lot of exotic local fish, here are the names of a few more common varieties:

| | | |
|---|---|---|
| أنشوجـة | ænshūgæ | anchovies |
| استاكوزا [كركند] | istækōzæ [kærækænd] | lobster |
| جمبرى [ قرادس ] | gæmbæri ['ærādis] | shrimp |
| جندفلى [معـار ] | gændofli [maḥḥār] | oysters |
| كابوريـا | kæboryæ | crab |
| سردين | særdīn | sardines |
| تونـة | tūnæ | tunny (tuna) |
| سمك موسى | sæmæk mūsæ | sole |

Some of the ways you may want your fish served:

| | | |
|---|---|---|
| baked | فى الفرن | fil forn |
| cured | مملح | momællæḥ |
| fried | مقـلى | mæ'li |
| grilled | مشوى | mæshwi |
| marinated | متبَّـل | motæbbæl |
| poached | مسلـوق | mæslū' |
| smoked | مـدخن | modækhkhæn |
| steamed | بالبغـار | bil bokhār |

| | |
|---|---|
| كبـاب سمك (kæbāb sæmæk) | chunks of fish, stewed and charcoal grilled with pieces of tomatoes and green pepper |
| سمك صيادية (sæmæk sayyadiyyæ) | chunks of fish cooked in oil and served with rice flavoured with the fish cooking oil |

## Meat

Eating pork is forbidden according to Moslem dietary laws, therefore it's rarely found on a menu.

| | | |
|---|---|---|
| What kinds of meat do you have? | أى أصناف اللحم عندكم ؟ | ʾæyy ʾasnāf ællæḥm ʾændokom |
| I'd like some... | أريد لحم ... | orīd læḥm |
| beef/veal/lamb | بقرى/بتلو/ضانى | bæʿæri/bitillo/dāni |

| Arabic | Transliteration | English |
|---|---|---|
| أوزى | ʾūzi | baby lamb |
| ريش [كستليتة] ضانى | riyæsh [kostælētæ] dāni | lamb chops |
| لسان | lisæn | tongue |
| اسكالوب | ʾiskælop | scallop |
| جامبون – خنزير | zhæmbōn-khænzīr | ham |
| كوارع بتلو | kæwæriʿ bitillo | calf's trotters (feet) |
| لحم مفروم | læḥm mafrūm | minced meat |
| كستليتة | kostælētæ | cutlets |
| موزة | mōzæ | shank, knuckle |
| سجق [مقانق] | sogoʿ [mæʿænik] | sausages |
| كستليتة بتلو [عجل] | kostælētæ bitillo [ʾigl] | veal chops |
| بفتيك | boftēk | beef steak |
| فغذ (ضانى) | fækhdæ (dāni) | leg (of lamb) |
| مخ | mokh | brains |
| كلاوى | kælæwi | kidneys |
| كتف | kitf | shoulder |
| روسبيف | rozbīf | roast beef |
| رأس [نيفة] | rās [nīfæ] | head |
| رقبة | ræʿæbæ | neck |
| فيلتو | filitto | fillet |
| صدر | sidr | breast |
| كبدة | kibdæ | liver |
| كفتة | koftæ | meatballs |
| كرشة | kirshæ | tripe |

## Arabic meat dishes

كبـاب
(kæbǣb)

spicy chunks of charcoal-grilled lamb

ريش
(riyæsh)

spicy charcoal-grilled lamb chops

كفـتة
(koftæ)

charcoal-grilled minced meatballs

شاورمـة
(shawirmæ)

chunks of lamb roasted on a vertical spit from
which thin slices are cut and served either
in a bun or on a plate, usually with rice;
a popular snack served from roadside stands

كبيبة [ كبـة ]
(kobēbæ [kibbæ])

minced meat, cracked wheat, onion, baked
in butter; it can be served raw *(kobeiba naya)*,
baked *(kobeiba besseniyah)* or rolled into
dumplings and served in goat's milk soup
*(kobeiba labniyeh)* (Lebanon)

مقلـوبة
(mæ'lūbæ)

meat and aubergine (eggplant) served with rice

فتـة
(fættæ)

boiled mutton and rice mixed with bread
crumbs and broth, served with vinegar and
garlic

صفيحـة
(sfīhæ)

a pastry crust like pizza garnished with
seasoned minced mutton (Lebanon)

| | | |
|---|---|---|
| barbecued | مشوى على الفحم | mæshwi 'ælæl fæḥm |
| fried | مقلـى | mæ'li |
| grilled | مشوى | mæshwi |
| roasted | رستـو | rosto |
| stewed | مسلـوق | mæslū' |
| stuffed | محشى | mæḥshi |
| underdone (rare) | قليـل السواء | kalil ælsiwæ |
| medium | نصف سواء | nisf siwæ |
| well-done | مستـوى | mistiwi |

# Game and fowl

I'd like some game.

أريد طيـور . orīd toyūr

| أرنب | 'ærnæb | rabbit |
|---|---|---|
| بط | batt | duck |
| بط بـرِّى | batt bærri | wild duck |
| حمـام | hæmæm | pigeon |
| ديك رومى [حبشى] | dīk rūmi [ḥæbæsh] | turkey |
| سمان [سمـن] | simmæn [sommon] | quail |
| فراخ [فراريج] | firækh [frærizh] | chicken |
| ورك/صدر/كبدة | wirk/sidr/kibdæ | leg/breast/liver |
| فراخ [فراريج] مشوية | firækh [frærizh] mæshwiyyæ | roast chicken |
| وز | wizz | goose |

# Game and poultry dishes

فراخ شركسية
(firækh shærkæsiyyæ)

boiled chicken served with boiled rice and a sauce made of chopped walnuts, chili pepper and bread

فراخ بالخلطة
(firækh bil khalta)

roast chicken served with rice mixed with nuts, chicken liver and giblets

كشك بالفراخ
(kishk bil firækh)

pieces of boiled chicken braised in a gravy made of yogurt, chicken broth, onion and butter

حمام معشى أرز/فريك
(hæmæm mæḥshi roz/firīk)

pigeon stuffed with cracked wheat or seasoned rice

برام حمـام
(biræm ḥæmæm)

pigeon baked in a casserole with rice and milk (Egypt)

## Vegetables

| | | |
|---|---|---|
| What vegetables do you recommend ? | بأىّ الخضروات تنصح ؟ | bi'æyy ælkhodrawāt tænsaḥ |
| أرز | roz | rice |
| باذنجان | bitingāēn | aubergine (eggplant) |
| باميـة | bæmyæ | okra |
| باذلاء [ بسلــة ] | bisillæ | peas |
| بصـــل | basal | onions |
| بطاطس | batātis | potatoes |
| ثـــوم | tōm | garlic |
| جرجير | gærgīr | watercress |
| جزر | gazar | carrots |
| حمص | hommos | chick-peas |
| خرشوف [ أرضى شوكى ] | kharshūf [ardi shōki] | artichoke |
| خس | khass | lettuce |
| خيــار | khiyār | cucumber |
| ذرة | dora | Indian corn |
| سبانخ | sæbāēnikh | spinach |
| طرشى [ كبيس ] | torshi [kæbīs] | gherkins |
| طماطم [ بندورة ] | tamātim [banadūra] | tomatoes |
| عــدس | 'æds | lentils |
| فاصوليــا | fasolya | beans |
| لوبيا/خضراء/فول | lobyæ/khadra/fūl | string/green/black |
| فريـــك | firīk [borgol] | cracked wheat |
| فجـــل | figl | radishes |
| فلفـــل أخضر | filfil akhdar | green peppers |
| قنبيط (أرنبيط) | arnabit | cauliflower |
| كرفس | karafs | celery |
| كرنب [ملفوف] | koromb [mælfūf] | cabbage |
| ورق عنب | wæræ' 'inæb | grape leaves |

Vegetables may be served:

| baked | فى الفرن | fil forn |
| boiled | مسلوق | mæslū' |
| chopped | مخرط | mikharrat |
| creamed | بالصلصة البيضاء | bil **salsa** ælbēda |
| diced | مكعبـات | mokæ'æ **bāt** |
| fried | مقـلى | mæ'li |
| grilled | مشوى | mæshwi |
| roasted | رستـو | rosto |
| stewed | مسلـوق | mosæbbæk |
| stuffed | محشى | mæḥshi |

## Vegetable dishes

**ملوخيـة**
(molokhiyyæ)

A very popular Egyptian dish is a spicy soup of greens flavoured with garlic. It's usually made with rice and chicken or meat.

**مسقعـة**
(mosækkæ'æ)

Fried aubergine (eggplant) cooked with meat and raisins

**محشى**
(mæḥshi)

There's a variety of vegetables which fall into the category of *mahshees*. These are stuffed with a mixture of chopped meat (usually lamb or mutton), rice, onion and herbs. The most popular *mahshees* are the ones with grape leaves, green peppers, cabbage leaves, marrows (US zucchini), tomatoes and aubergine (eggplant). They can be eaten hot or cold and are usually served with yogurt.

**لوبيـا بزيت**
(lūbyæ bzēt)

Green beans fried in oil, then braised in tomato sauce and served chilled with lemon (Lebanon)

**باميـة بالموزة**
(bæmyæ bil mōzæ)

Okra braised in tomato sauce with beef knuckle

## Fool

*Fool* is doubtless the favourite food preparation in the Middle East; its widespread popularity and its price put it on par with a hot-dog. *Fool* consists of black beans which have been cooked the previous night, seasoned with oil and lemon juice or served with butter. It may be served on a plate or in a bun. If you're in a hurry, stop at any *fool* restaurant and buy a *fool* or *falafel* sandwich.

| | |
|---|---|
| فلافــل<br>(fælǣfil) | small balls of ground fool, mixed with greens and spices, fried in oil |
| بسارة<br>(bisāra) | a purée made of ground fool, cooked with butter, and served with fried onions |

*Fool* may also be eaten with Arab bread. Made of wheat- and Indian corn-flour, this tasty, flat, round bread replaces eating with utensils as it's used to scoop up food right from the bowl or plate.

## Seeds, nuts, dried fruit

A major pastime in the Middle East seems to be cracking seeds. They're sold everywhere—near stadiums, at the cinema, on the streets and in the markets. The most common seed is from a variety of melon. Vendors of dried seeds also offer a choice of nuts and dried fruit.

| dried seeds | محمصات | moḥammasāt |
|---|---|---|
| chestnuts | أبو فروة [ كاستنة ] | ʼæbū farwa [kæstænæ] |
| pecans | بكـان | pikkǣn |
| hazelnuts | بنـدق | bondoʼ |
| nuts | جـوز | gōz |
| walnuts | عين جمــل | ʼēn gæmæl |
| pistachio | فستق | fostoʼ |
| peanuts | فول سودانى | fūl sūdǣni |
| almonds | لــوز | lōz |

# Fruit

The mild climate permits the cultivation of most of the fruit known in Europe as well as those from the tropics.

| | | |
|---|---|---|
| Do you have fresh fruit? | هل عندكم فواكه طازة ؟ | hæl ændokom fæwǣkih tāza |
| أنــانـاس | 'ænænā̄s | pineapple |
| برتقال [ليمون] | borto'ā̄n [læymūn] | orange |
| برقوق [خوخ] | bær'ū' [khōkh] | plums |
| بطيخ | battīkḥ | watermelon |
| بلح | bælæh | dates |
| تفـاح | tiffā̄ḥ | apples |
| تين | tin | figs |
| جريب فروت | grēb frūt | grapefruit |
| جوافة | gæwā̄fæ | guava |
| جوز هندى | gōz hind | coconut |
| خوخ [دراء] | khōkh [darrā'] | peach |
| رمـان | rommā̄n | pomegranates |
| زبيب | zibīb | raisins |
| شمـام | shæmmā̄m | melon |
| عنب (بنـاتى) | 'inæb (bænā̄ti) | (seedless) grapes |
| فراولة | frawla | strawberries |
| قشطـة خضراء | 'ishta khadra | custard apple, papaw |
| كـريز | krēz | cherries |
| كمثرى [نجاص] | kommitræ [nzhās] | pear |
| ليمون [حامض] | læmūn [ḥāmid] | lime |
| ليمون حلو | læmūn ḥilw | sweet lemon |
| مـانجة | mængæ | mangoes |
| مشمش | mishmish | apricots |
| مـوز | mōz | banana |
| يوسفندى [أفندى] | yosæfændi ['æfændi] | tangerines |

## Dessert

If you've survived all the courses on the menu, you may want to say:

| | | |
|---|---|---|
| I'd like a dessert, please. | أريد حلوا من فضلك . | orīd ḥilw min fadlak |
| Something light, please. | شيء خفيف من فضلك . | shē' khæfīf min fadlak |
| Just a small portion. | مقدار صغير . | mikdār sagīr |
| Nothing more, thanks. | لا شيء آخر ، شكرأ . | læ shē' 'ākhar shokran |

If you aren't sure what to order, ask the waiter:

| | | |
|---|---|---|
| What do you have for dessert? | أى حلويات عندكم ؟ | 'æyy hælæwiyyǣt ændokom |
| What do you recommend? | بم تنصح ؟ | bimæ tansaḥ |
| cake | كيــك | kēk |
| caramel custard | كريم كراميــل | krēm karamil |
| fruit salad | فروت سالاد | frūt salad |
| ice-cream | أيس كريم | 'ǣys krim |
| rice pudding | أرز بلبن | roz bilæbæn |
| water-ice (sherbet) | جرانيطة [ بوظة ] | grānīta [būza] |

Arabs have a sweet tooth for gooey, syrupy desserts like the well-known *baklava*. Some desserts even bear such fascinating names as Lady's Navel and Ali's Mother. These desserts are usually served with cream. If not, you can ask for your dessert:

| | | |
|---|---|---|
| with cream | بقشطــة | bi'ishta |

Here are some favourite Arabic desserts:

| | |
|---|---|
| بسيمــة (bæsimæ) | semolina pudding baked with coconut and sugar |

بقـلاوة
(bæklǣwæ)
thin layers of pastry, filled with nuts, almonds and pistachios, steeped in syrup

بلح الشــام
(bælæḥ ishshǣm)
"Syria's dates": puff pastry, fried, steeped in syrup

خشاف
(khoshǣf)
stewed fruit

صرة الست
(sorrit issit)
"lady's navel": a ring-shaped sweet, steeped in syrup

عيش السراى
('ēsh æl sarāyæ)
"palace bread": deep-fried sweet roll, steeped in syrup

قـرع عسلى
(kar' 'æsæli)
pumpkin pudding with nuts, covered with a vanilla sauce; may be served hot or chilled

قطــايف
(katāyif)
a pastry filled with nuts, fried and then topped with syrup

كــل واشكر
(kol woshkor)
"eat it and thank God": smaller version of *baklava*, with less crust and more nuts, steeped in syrup

كنــافة
(konǣfæ)
pastry of thin fibres, baked with nuts or cream, steeped in syrup

أم على
(om ali)
"Ali's mother", named after an Egyptian Mameluke queen; raisin cake, steeped in milk

بسبـوسة
(bæsbūsæ)
semolina tart, baked with butter, covered with syrup

مهلبيـة
(mæhællæbiyyæ)
rice or Indian corn-flour pudding

ملبن [لكـوم]
(mælbæn [lokūm])
Turkish delight

After a dinner including dessert and fruit, Arabs like to drink a cup of Turkish coffee. You'll certainly want to sample this world-renowned brew which will probably be the only type of coffee you'll be able to find. Turkish coffee is quite strong. It's boiled up three or more times in small, long-handled pots. When the coffee is served—grounds and all—let it sit a minute so that the grounds can settle to the bottom of the cup, and then sip only half the cup. You'll have to let the waiter know in advance whether or not you want your coffee sweetened, as the sugar and coffee are brewed together. Milk, sugar or cream aren't served with the coffee. Ask for:

| | | |
|---|---|---|
| Turkish coffee | قهوة تركى | 'æhwæ torki |

And according to how much sugar you want, say:

| | | |
|---|---|---|
| very sweet | سكر زيادة | sokkar ziyāēdæ |
| medium | مضبوط | mazbūt |
| without sugar | سادة | sāēdæ |

That's the end of our Arabic menu. For wine and other drinks, see the following pages. But after the feast comes...

## The bill (check)

| | | |
|---|---|---|
| May I have the bill (check), please? | . أريد الحساب من فضلك | orīd æl ḥisāēb min fadlak |
| Haven't you made a mistake? | ألا توجد غلطة ؟ | 'ælāē tūgæd galta |
| Is service included? | هل هذا يشمل الخدمة ؟ | hæl hāēzæ yæshmæl æl khidmæ |
| Is everything included? | هل هذا يشمل كل شىء ؟ | hæl hāēzæ yæshmæl koll shē' |
| Do you accept traveller's cheques? | هل تقبـل الشيكات السياحية ؟ | hæl takbæl æl shēkāēt æl siyāēḥiyyæ |
| Thank you, this is for you. | . شكراً ، هذا لك | shokran hāēzæ læk |
| Keep the change. | . احتفظ بالبـاقى | 'iḥtafiz bil bāki |

| | | |
|---|---|---|
| That was a very good meal. We enjoyed it. Thank you. | كان الأكل عظيماً وأعجبنا جداً . شكراً . | kāēnæl 'ækl azim wæ æægæbænā giddæn shokran |
| We'll come again sometime. | سنأتي مرة ثانية ان شاء الله . | sænæ'ti marra tænyæ 'in shā'allāh |

---

الخدمة محسوبة

SERVICE INCLUDED

---

## Complaints

But perhaps you'll have something to complain about...

| | | |
|---|---|---|
| That's not what I ordered. I asked for... | هذا ليس ما طلبته . أنا طلبت ... | hāēzæ læysæ mæ talabto. 'ænā talabt |
| I don't like this/ I can't eat this. | هذا لا يعجبني / لا يمكن أن آكل هذا . | hāēzæ lāē yo'giboni/læ yomkin 'æn 'āēkol hāēzæ |
| May I change this? | هل يمكن تغيير هذا ؟ | hæl yomkin tægyir hāēzæ |
| The meat is... | اللحم ... | æl læhm |
| overdone | شديد السواء | shæēdid æl siwæ |
| underdone | قليل السواء | kalīl æl siwæ |
| too tough | ناشف جـداً | nāēshif giddæn |
| This is too... | هذا ... جداً . | hāēzæ... giddæn |
| bitter/salty/sweet | مرّ / مالح / مسكر | morr/māēlih/misakkar |
| The food is cold. | الأكل بارد . | æl 'ækl bāērid |
| This isn't fresh. | هذا ليس طازة . | hāēzæ læysæ tāza |
| Would you ask the head waiter to come over? | اطلب من المتر الحضور من فضلك . | otlob minæl mitr æl hodūr min fadlak |

60

## Drinks

### Beer

Beer has been drunk in the Middle East as far back as the
ancient Egyptians and Mesopotamians. Good beer is still
brewed in the Middle East, and today in Egypt you can ask
for Stella beer (**bi**ræ **stil**læ), a light, lager beer, or an Aswan
beer (**bi**rit as**wān**), a dark beer; Almaza (al**ma**za) and Laziza
(la**zi**za) are noted brands in Lebanon.

### Wine

The Middle East was doubtless the birthplace of wine. From
biblical times to the eighth century A.D., vineyards flour-
ished. But Islam forbids the drinking of wine, and production was sharply curtailed. In the last century, however,
wine production was stepped up considerably.

The wine cellars of Ksara in Lebanon, founded by the
Jesuits in 1857, are the largest in the Middle East. Egypt's
Gianaclis vineyards on the Nile Delta at Abu Hummus are
noted. Most of the wine is white but among the red is the
remarkable Omar Khayyam which is full-bodied and has a
curious aftertaste of dates.

You'll only be able to order wine in large restaurants, especially those specializing in foreign dishes catering to foreign
clientele.

| | | |
|---|---|---|
| Omar Khayyam (red) | عمر خيــام | omar khæyyā̈m |
| Ptolemy (white) | نبيذ البطــالسة | nibīt æl batalsæ |
| Matameer (red) | نبيذ المطامير | nibīt æl matamīr |
| Gianaclis (red or white) | نبيذ جناكليس | nibīt zhænæklīs |
| Queen Cleopatra (white) | نبيذ كليوباترة | nibīt kilyobatra |
| Pharaoh's Wine (red) | نبيذ الفراعنة | nibit æl fara'na |

| | | |
|---|---|---|
| I'd like ... of wine. | أريد ... نبيذ . | orid ... nibīt |
| a bottle | زجـاجة | zogǣgit |
| half a bottle | نصف زجاجة | nisf zogǣgit |
| a glass | كبـاية | kobbæyit |
| I'd like something... | أريد شيئاً ... | orid shæy'æn |
| sweet/sparkling/dry | حلواً/بغازات/جافا | ḥilw/bigǣzǣt/gǣf |
| I want a bottle of white wine. | أريد زجاجة نبيذ أبيض . | orid zogǣgit nibīt 'abyad |

| | | |
|---|---|---|
| red | أحمر | 'aḥmar |
| white | أبيض | 'abyad |
| rosé | روزيه | rozē |

| | | |
|---|---|---|
| I don't want anything too sweet. | لا أريد شيئاً حلواً جداً . | lǣ orīd shē' ḥilw giddæn |
| How much is a bottle of...? | بكم زجاجة ... ؟ | bikæm zogǣgit |
| Haven't you anything cheaper? | هل عندك شيء أرخص ؟ | hæl 'ændæk shē' arkhas |
| Fine, that'll do. | هذا حسن . | hǣzæ ḥæsæn |

## If you enjoyed the wine, you may want to say:

| | | |
|---|---|---|
| Bring me another... please. | أريد ... آخر من فضلك . | orid ... 'ākhar min fadlak |
| glass/bottle | كوب / زجاجة | kūb/zogǣgæ |
| What's the name of this wine? | ما اسم هذا النبيذ ؟ | mǣ 'ism hǣzæ æl nibīt |
| Where does this wine come from? | من أين يأتى هذا النبيذ ؟ | min 'æynæ yæ'ti hǣzæ æl nibīt |
| How old is this wine? | ما عمر هذا النبيذ ؟ | mǣ 'omr hǣzæ æl nibīt |

## Other beverages

If you want some bottled mineral water, ask for *Sehha,* a mineral water from Lebanon.

| | | |
|---|---|---|
| I'd like some mineral water/a bottle of *Sehha.* | أريد ميـاه معدنية / زجاجة صحة . | orīd miyāēh mæ'dæniyyæ/ zogāēgit siḥḥa |

With the great abundance of fruit available, fruit juice is a very popular drink in the Arab countries. Don't miss the opportunity to stop at one of the stands selling fruit juice which will be freshly squeezed for you. Lemon, sugar-cane and mango juice are the favourites.

| | | |
|---|---|---|
| I'd like a/an ... juice. | أريد عصير ... | orīd asīr |
| apricot | مشمش | mishmish |
| carrot | جـزر | gazar |
| grape | عنب | 'inæb |
| guava | جوافـة | gæwāēfæ |
| lemon | ليمون [ حامض ] | læmūn [ḥāmid] |
| mango | مـانجو | mængæ |
| orange | برتقـال | borto'āēn |
| pomegranate | رمـان | rommān |
| strawberry | فراولـة | frawla |
| sugar-cane | قصب سكر | 'asab sokkar |
| tamarind | تمر هنـدى | tamr hindi |

A popular figure in Egypt is the *erkesoos* vendor, who walks the streets dressed in a colourful costume, calling attention to his presence by playing a type of finger bell. He'll gladly sell you a glass of *erkesoos* (a soft drink made from licorice) from the large bottle he carries. Just stop him and say:

| | | |
|---|---|---|
| I'd like a glass of *erkesoos,* please. | أريد كبـاية عرقسوس من فضلك . | orīd kobbāēyit 'irkisūs min fadlak |

# Coffee house

Going to a café in an Arab country is more than just for refreshment. It's a tradition. Inside or on the terrace, observing the drama of Arab street life, the atmosphere of the café is one of calm and cordiality.

While you can also order tea, soft drinks or mineral water, you'll undoubtedly want to try Turkish coffee. You've a choice: you can order it without sugar, sweet or very sweet.

Two other important activities in a café are smoking a water pipe or nargile and playing backgammon and dominoes. If you decide to try the water pipe, clap your hands to attract the waiter's attention, and ask him for a *nargile*. You'll have to tell him whether you want *tamback,* a natural coarse-cut tobacco, or *ma assil,* a lighter tobacco mixed with molasses.

The waiter will prepare the pipe and the tobacco, take the first puff to see that it's well lit, and then turn it over to you.

It's likely that a shoe-shine boy will offer to shine your shoes if you're a man but he won't do it for women!

When you're ready to leave, clap your hands and ask the waiter for the bill. For tipping, see inside back-cover.

| I'd like a cup of... | أريد فنجان . . . | orïd fingæn |
| coffee | قهـوة | 'æhwæ |
| tea | شــای | shæy |
| mint tea | شای بنعنـاع | shæy bini'nææ æ |
| I'd like a water pipe. | أريد شيشة [أرجيلة] . | orïd shishæ ['argïlæ] |
| Bring us a back-gammon board/some dominoes, please. | نريد طاولة / دومينو من فضلك . | norïd tawla/domino min fadlak |

FOR COFFEE, see also page 58

64

## Eating light—Snacks

Stopping for a snack is a very popular thing to do in Arab countries, especially since their equivalent to our snackbars are open nearly all night. So, after the cinema, a football game or a concert, you can stop at a snack-bar to sample *fool, falafel* or *shawerma.*

| | | |
|---|---|---|
| Give me two of these and one of those. | اعطيني ٢ من هذه و ١ من هذه . | 'aatini 'itnēn min hæzihi wæ wǣḥid min hǣzihi |
| to the left/to the right | الى الشمال / الى اليمين | 'ilæ æshshimǣl/'ilæl yæmīn |
| above/below | الى أعلى / الى أسفل | 'ilæ 'æælǣ/'ilæ 'æsfæl |
| I'd like a/an/some…, please. | أريد … من فضلك . | orīd… min fadlak |
| cheese sandwich | سندوتش جبنة | sændæwitsh gibnæ |
| liver sandwich | سندوتش كبدة | sændæwitsh kibdæ |
| sausage sandwich | سندوتش سجق [معانق] | sændæwitsh sogo' [mæ'ǣnik] |
| roast beef sandwich | سندوتش روسبيف | sændæwitsh rozbīf |
| tongue sandwich | سندوتش لسان | sændæwitsh lisǣn |
| chicken sandwich | سندوتش فراخ | sændæwitsh firǣkh |
| baked macaroni, served with white sauce | مكرونة بالفرن | makarōna bil forn |
| bread | خبز | khobz |
| butter | زبدة | zibdæ |
| cake | كيك | kēk |
| hamburger | همبرجر | hamborgar |
| ice-cream | أيس كريم | 'ǣys krim |
| pastry | حلويات | ḥælæwiyyǣt |
| salad | صلاطة | salata |
| How much is that? | بكم هذا ؟ | bikæm hǣzæ |

# Travelling around

The principal cities of Egypt—Cairo, Alexandria, Luxor and Aswan—are linked by regular flights. Because of their small area, Lebanon and Jordan aren't served by any domestic flights. At any airport you're sure to find someone who speaks English.

| | | |
|---|---|---|
| Do you speak English? | هل تتكلم الانجليزية ؟ | hæl tætækællam ingilīzi |
| Is there a flight to Amman? | هل توجد رحلة الى عمان ؟ | hæl tūgæd riḥlæ ilæ 'æmmæn |
| When's the next plane to Cairo? | ما موعد الطائرة القادمة الى القاهرة ؟ | mæ mæw'id æl tā'ira æl kādimæ ilæ ælkāhira |
| Can I make a connection to Beirut? | هل أستطيع أن أعمل امتداد الى بيروت ؟ | hæl astatī æn æ'mil 'imtidæd ilæ bæyrūt |
| I'd like a ticket to Damascus. | أريد تذكرة لدمشق . | orīd tæzkara li dimishk |
| What's the fare to Luxor? | ما الثمن الى الأقصر ؟ | mæ æl tæmæn ilæ loksor |
| single (one-way) | ذهاب | zihæb |
| return (roundtrip) | ذهاب واياب | zihæb wæ 'iyæb |
| What time does the plane take off? | متى تقوم الطائرة ؟ | mætæ tækūm æl tā'ira |
| What time do I have to check in? | متى يجب أن أقدم نفسى فى المطار ؟ | mætæ yægib æn okaddim næfsi fil matār |
| What's the flight number? | ما نمرة الرحلة ؟ | mæ nimrit æl riḥlæ |
| What time do we arrive? | متى نصل ؟ | mætæ nasill |

| | |
|---|---|
| وصـــول <br> ARRIVAL | رحيـــل <br> DEPARTURE |

## Bus

Buses and taxis are the most important means of transportation in the Middle East. City buses provide a regular, if crowded, service. Cities are linked by ordinary and express services. Express buses are comfortable and very reasonably priced.

It isn't advisable to travel by bus in the big cities during the rush hours: buses are so overcrowded that you would have to hang on to the outside! If you are in Lebanon it might be better to try a collective taxi (called a *service*—sær**vis**—in Arabic). A *service* will wait until it's full, and will then follow the regular bus route. These collective taxis operate in all major cities. Only slightly more expensive than the bus, they are often more convenient.

In Egypt collective taxis ply between Cairo and Alexandria. They leave from the railway station.

City buses show their destinations in Arabic and their route numbers in our figures. When you plan to take a bus the best thing is to ask your hotel desk clerk for directions.

City buses don't follow any set schedule. Buses run frequently, so just go to the bus stop and wait. Your bus is bound to come along soon. Interurban buses, on the other hand, do have time-tables.

## Inquiries

| | | |
|---|---|---|
| I'd like a bus pass. | أريد اشتراك أوتوبيس . | or**i**d ish**t**ir**ā**k otob**ī**s |
| Where can I get a bus/a collective taxi to...? | أين أجد أوتوبيس / تاكسى مشترك الى ... ؟ | ayn**æ** 'æg**i**d otob**ī**s/t**æ**ksi mosh**t**arak 'il**æ** |
| What bus do I take to Abou-Kir? | أى أوتوبيس أركب الى أبى قير ؟ | **æ**yy otob**ī**s **æ**rk**æ**b il**æ** 'æb**ū**k**i**r |

FOR TAXI, see page 27

| What number is it to...? | ؟... ما النمرة للذهاب الى | mæ æl **nimr**æ lil **zih**æb ilæ |
| Where's the...? | ؟ ... أين | æynæ |
| bus station | موقف الأوتوبيس | **mawkif** æl 'oto**bīs** |
| bus stop | محطة الأوتوبيس | ma**hatt**it æl 'oto**bīs** |
| When's the ... bus to Amman? | متى يقوم الأوتوبيس ؟ الى عمان ... | mætæ ya**kūm** æl 'oto**bīs**... ilæ 'æmm**ā**n ? |
| first/last/next | الأول / الأخير / القادم | æl 'æww**æ**l/æl 'æ**khīr**/æl **kā**dim |
| Do I have to change buses? | هل يجب أن أغير الأوتوبيس ؟ | hæl **yægib** æn o**gæyyir** æl 'oto**bīs** |
| How long does the journey take? | ؟ ما مدة الرحلة | mæ **moddit** æl **rihl**æ |

## Tickets

| Where's the information office? | ؟ أين مكتب الاستعلامات | æynæ **mækt**æb æl 'isti'læ**māt** |
| Where can I buy a ticket? | ؟ أين أشترى التذكرة | æynæ æsh**tæri** æl **tazkara** |
| I want a ticket to Cairo. | . أريد تذكرة للقاهرة | o**rīd** tazkara lil **kā**hira |
| I'd like 2 singles to El Mansura.* | أريد تذكرتين ذهاب للمنصورة . | o**rīd** tazkar**tēn** zihæb lil man**sūra** |
| How much is the fare to Alexandria? | ؟ بكم التذكرة للاسكندرية | bi**kæm** æl tazkara lil 'æskændæ**riyy**æ |
| Is it half price for a child? He's/She's 13. | هل أدفع نصف تذكرة للطفل ؟ سنه/سنها ١٣سنة. | hæl æd**fæ**' nisf tazkara lil tifl? **sinno/sinnæh**æ 13 **sæn**æ |

*Note:* Children up to the age of five travel free.

* see grammar

FOR NUMBERS, see page 175

| | |
|---|---|
| ذهاب أم ذهاب واياب ؟ | Single or return (one-way or roundtrip)? |
| تدفع نصف تذكرة حتى سن . . . | It's half price up to the age of... |
| يجب أن تدفع تذكرة كاملة. | You'll have to pay full fare. |

## All aboard

| | | |
|---|---|---|
| Excuse me. May I get by? | آسف . أريد المرور . | æsif. orīd æl morūr |
| Is this seat taken? | هل هذا الكرسى معجوز ؟ | hæl hæzæl korsi mæḥgūz |
| Is this seat free? | هل هذا الكرسى فاضى ؟ | hæl hæzæl korsi fādi |

ممنوع التدخين
NO SMOKING

| | | |
|---|---|---|
| I think that's my seat. | أظن أن هذا الكرسى لى . | azonn ænnæ hæzæl korsi li |
| Can you tell me when we get to Memphis? | متى نصل الى ممفيس من فضلك ؟ | mætæ nasil ilæ mæmfis min fadlak |
| What station is this? | ما هذه المحطة ؟ | mæ hæzihi æl maḥatta |
| Will you tell me when to get off? | قل لى متى أنزل من فضلك . | 'olli mætæ ænzil min fadlak |
| I want to get off at Khan El-Khalili. | أريد النزول عند خان الغليلى . | orīd æl nozūl inda khæn ælkhælili |
| Please let me off at the next stop. | من فضلك أنزلنى فى المحطة الجاية . | min fadlak ænzilni fil maḥatta æl gæyyæ |
| May I have my luggage, please? | أريد شنطتى من فضلك . | orīd shantiti min fadlak |

## Train

What few passenger trains run in Jordan and Lebanon are
slow and uncomfortable. Egypt, on the other hand, has a
modern railway system with express trains. Fares are cheap,
and trains are comfortable. During high season, it's advisable to reserve seats ahead of time.

Trains in Egypt generally have a dining-car, while sometimes hot meals can be served right at your seat. The steward
will pass through the car to take your order. Usually, there's
a set menu. You can also order drinks and sandwiches from
him.

If you're in a hurry, take an air conditioned express train
(with first and second class) which links major cities. For
long trips, you can reserve a berth or compartment in a
sleeping-car.

Children travel free up to the age of five and pay half-fare
from six to ten. Note that at the railway station, ticket win-
dows are segregated according to sex—and that the queue
for women is generally shorter...

| | | |
|---|---|---|
| درجة أولى | FIRST CLASS | |
| درجة ثانية | SECOND CLASS | |

## To the station

| | | |
|---|---|---|
| Where's the railway station? | أين محطة السكة الحديد ؟ | æynæ maḥattit æl sikkæ æl ḥædid |
| Taxi, please! | تاكسى ! | tæksi |
| Take me to the railway station. | خذنى الى محطة السكة الحديد . | khodni ilæ maḥattit æl sikkæ æl ḥædid |

## Inquiries

| How much is the fare to Suez? | ؟ بكم التذكرة الى السويس | bikæm æl **taz**kara ilǣ ælsiwēs |
| Is it a through train? | ؟ هل هو قطار مباشر | hæl howæ ki**ṭ**ār mobǣshir |
| Does the train stop at Al Minya? | ؟ هل يتوقف القطار فى المنيا | hæl yætæ**wakk**af æl kitār fil **min**yæ |
| When is the ... train to Aswan? | متى يقوم القطار ... الى أسوان ؟ | mætǣ yæ**kūm** æl kitār ... ilǣ as**wān** |
| first/last/next | الأول / الأخير / القادم | æl 'æwwæl/æl 'ækhīr/æl **kā**dim |
| What time does the train from Damascus arrive? | متى يصل القطار القادم من دمشق ؟ | mætǣ **ya**sil æl kitār æl **kā**dim min di**mishk** |
| What time does the train for Alexandria leave? | ؟متى يقوم قطار الاسكندرية | mætǣ yakūm kitār æl 'æskændæ**riyy**æ |
| Is the train late? | ؟ هل القطار متأخر | hæl æl kitār motæ'**ækhkh**ir |
| Is there a dining-car/ sleeping-car on the train? | هل توجد فى القطار عربة طعام / عربة نوم ؟ | hæl **tū**gæd fil kitār 'arabit ta'**ām**/'arabit nōm |

| دخول | ENTRANCE |
| خروج | EXIT |
| الى الرصيف | TO THE PLATFORMS |

## Platform (track)

| What platform does the train for Suez leave from? | من أى رصيف يقوم قطار السويس ؟ | min æyy ra**sif** yakūm kitār ælsiwēs |
| Where is platform 4? | ؟ أين رصيف ٤ | æynæ rasif 4 |
| Is this the right platform for the train to Port-Saïd? | هل هذا هو الرصيف المضبوط لقطار بور سعيد ؟ | hæl **hǣ**zæ howæ æl rasif æl maz**būt** likitār bōr sa'**īd** |

FOR TAXI, see page 27

| | |
|---|---|
| انه قطار مباشر . | It's a direct train. |
| يجب أن تغير فى ... | You have to change at... |
| درجة أولى أم ثانية ؟ | First or second class? |
| رصيف ... موجود ... | Platform ... is ... |
| هناك / تحت | over there/downstairs |
| على الشمال / على اليمين | on the left/on the right |
| قطار ... يقوم الساعة ...<br>على رصيف ... | The train to ... will leave at ...<br>from platform ... |

## Where's the ... ?

| | | |
|---|---|---|
| Where's the...? | أين ... ؟ | æynæ |
| left luggage office | مكتب الأمانات | mæktæb æl 'æmænāēt |
| lost property (lost and found) office | مكتب المفقودات | mæktæb æl mæfkūdāēt |
| newsstand | كشك الجرائد | koshk æl garā'id |
| restaurant | مطعم | mat'am |
| ticket office | شباك التذاكر | shibbāēk æl tæzāēkir |
| waiting room | صالة الانتظار | sālit æl intizār |

## Boat

Boats and steamers ply up and down the Nile. A trip on one of these magnificent, luxury steamers is well worthwhile. These boats are very chic and comfortable. You can take a relaxing one- or two-week cruise on one of them. From Cairo to Luxor takes about two weeks while the voyage from Aswan to Luxor or vice-versa lasts about a week.

The steamers put in at several ports, affording the opportunity to make land excursions. Tickets sold through travel

FOR TICKETS, see page 67

agents include full board on the ship plus an air ticket from Cairo to Aswan or Luxor. Local travel agents will advise you about sailing dates, which are usually once weekly or every two weeks.

There's also a one-day excursion by hydrofoil from Aswan to the ancient temple of Abu-Simbel with its enormous statue of Ramses II. Enquire about it at your hotel or travel agent's. In Cairo you can take a water-bus which you'll find quite pleasant.

| | | |
|---|---|---|
| When's the next steamer sailing for Luxor? | متى تقوم الباخرة القادمة الى الأقصر ؟ | mætætækūm ælbækhira æl kādimæ ilæ loksor |
| I'd like to book passage for 2 to Aswan.* | أريد أن أحجز تذكرتين لأسوان . | orīd æn æhgiz tæzkartēn li'aswān |
| I want a return (roundtrip) ticket on the hydrofoil to the Abu-Simbel temple. | أريد تذكرة ذهاب واياب الى معبد أبو سمبل على الهيدروفيل . | orīd tazkara zihæb wæ 'iyāb ilæ mæzæbæd abūsimbil ælæl hidrōfil |

## Other means of transportation

| | | |
|---|---|---|
| bicycle | عجلة [بسيكليت] | ægælæ [bisiklēt] |
| camelback riding | ركوب الجمل | rokūb æl gæmæl |
| helicopter | هليكوبتر | hilikobtar |
| hitchhiking | أوتوستوب | otostop |
| horseback riding | ركوب الخيل | rokūb æl khēl |
| moped (motorbike) | دراجة بخارية | darrāgæ bokhæriyyæ |
| motorcycle | موتوسيكل | motosikl |

And if you're really stuck, start...

| | | |
|---|---|---|
| walking | امشى | 'imshi |

* see grammar

# Around and about—Sightseeing

Here we're more concerned with the cultural aspect of life than with entertainment; and, for the moment, with towns rather than the countryside.

| English | Arabic | Transliteration |
|---|---|---|
| Can you recommend a good guide book on...? | من فضلك انصحني بدليـل سياحى جيد عن ... | min **fadlak** insaḥni bidælīl siyæḥi gæyyid ʼæn |
| Where's the tourist office? | أين مكتب السياحة ؟ | æynæ **mæk**tæb æl siyæ̃ḥæ |
| What are the main points of interest? | ما أهم المعالم السياحية ؟ | mæ̃ ʼæ**hæm** æl mæʼæ̃lim æl siyæ̃ḥiyyæ |
| We're here for... | سنبقى هنا ... | sænabkā honæ̃ |
| only a few hours | بضعة ساعات فقط | bidʼat sæ̃ʼæ̃t fakat |
| a day | يـوم | yōm |
| 3 days | ٣ أيـام | 3 æyyæ̃m |
| a week | أسبوع | osbū |
| Can you recommend a (city) sightseeing tour? | من فضلك انصحني بجولة سياحية (للمدينة) . | min **fadlak** insaḥni bigæwlæ siyæ̃ḥiyyæ (lilmædīnæ) |
| Where does the bus start from? | من أين يبدأ الأوتوبيس ؟ | min æynæ yæbdæʼ æl ʼotobis |
| Will it pick us up at the hotel? | هل سيأخذنا من الفندق ؟ | hæl sæyæ**ʼkhoz**næ̃ min æl fondok |
| What bus/tram (street-car) should we take? | ما الأوتوبيس / الترام الذى نركبه ؟ | mæ̃ æl ʼotobis/æl tirām ællæzi nærkabo |
| How much does the tour cost? | ما ثمن الجولة ؟ | mæ̃ tæmæn æl gæwlæ |
| What time does the tour start? | متى تبدأ الجولة ؟ | mætæ̃ tæbdæʼ æl gæwlæ |
| We'd like to rent a car for the day. | نريد تأجير سيارة ليوم . | norīd tæʼgīr sayyāra liyōm |
| Is there an English-speaking guide? | هـل يوجد مرشد سياحى يتكلم الانجليزية ؟ | hæl yūgæd morshid siyæ̃ḥi yætækællæm æl ʼingiliziyyæ |

FOR TIME OF DAY, see page 178

74

| Where is/Where are the...? | أين ... ؟ | æynæ |
|---|---|---|
| abbey | الـدير | æl dēr |
| amusement park | مدينة الملاهى | mædīnæt æl mælǣhi |
| aquarium | حديقة الأسماك | ḥædīkat æl 'æsmǣk |
| art gallery | قاعـة الفنون | kā'æt æl fonūn |
| artists' quarter | حى الفنانين | ḥæyy æl fænnænin |
| bazaar | السوق [البازار] | æl sūk [æl bazār] |
| beach | الشاطىء | æl shāti' |
| botanical gardens | العديقة النباتية | æl ḥædīka æl næbǣttiyyæ |
| bridge | الكوبرى [الجسر] | æl kobri [æl zhisr] |
| building | المبـنى | æl mæbnǣ |
| business district | حى الأعمال | ḥæyy æl 'æ æmǣl |
| basilica | البازيليك | æl bæzilīk |
| castle | القصر | æl kasr |
| catacombs | سراديب الأموات | særædīb æl mæwtǣ |
| cathedral | الكاتدرائية | æl kǣtidrā'iyyæ |
| citadel | القلعـة | æl kalaa |
| city centre | وسط المدينة | wasat æl mædīnæ |
| city hall | مبنى المحافظة | mæbnǣ æl moḥāfza |
| church | الكنيسة | æl kænīsæ |
| concert hall | قاعة الموسيقى | ka'æt æl mosīka |
| convent | الدير | æl dēr |
| docks | أرصفة الميناء | arsifat æl mīnæ |
| downtown area | وسط المدينة | wasat æl mædīnæ |
| exhibition | المعرض | æl maarad |
| factory | المصنع | æl masnaa |
| fortress | الحصن | æl ḥisn |
| fountain | النافورة | æl nafūra |
| gardens | العدائق | æl ḥædǣ'ik |
| harbour | الميناء | æl mīnæ |
| lake | البحيرة | æl boḥæyra |
| library | المكتبة | æl mæktæbæ |

FOR ASKING THE WAY, see page 143

75

| market | السوق | æl sūk |
| monastery | الدير | æl dēr |
| monument | النصب التذكارى | æl nasb æl tizkāēri |
| mosque | الجامع | æl gāēmiʻ |
| museum | المتحف | æl mætḥāēf |
| observatory | المرصد | æl marsad |
| old city | المدينة القديمة | æl mædīnæ æl kadīmæ |
| opera house | دار الأوبرا | dār æl obirā |
| palace | القصر | æl kasr |
| park | الحديقة | æl ḥædīka |
| parliament building | مبنى البرلمان | mæbnāē æl barlamān |
| presidential palace | القصر الجمهورى | æl kasr æl gumhūri |
| pyramids | الأهرام | æl ahrām |
| river | النهر | æl nahr |
| royal palace | القصر الملكى | æl kasr æl mælæki |
| ruins | الأطلال | æl atlāl |
| seafront | شاطىء البحر | shāṭiʻ æl baḥr |
| shopping centre | المركز التجارى | æl mærkæz æl togāēri |
| sphinx | أبو الهول | abul hōl |
| stadium | الأستاد | æl ʼistāēd |
| statue | التمثال | æl timsāēl |
| stock exchange | البورصة | æl borsa |
| swimming pool | حمام السباحة [البسين] | hæmmāēm æl sibāēḥæ [pisīn] |
| synagogue | المعبد اليهودى | æl mææbæd æl yæhūdi |
| temple | المعبد | æl mææbæd |
| theatre | المسرح | æl masraḥ |
| tomb | القبر | æl kabr |
| tower | البرج | æl borg |
| university | الجامعة | æl gæmʻæ |
| walls | سور المدينة | sūr æl mædīnæ |
| zoo | حديقة الحيوان | ḥædīkat æl ḥæyæwāēn |

## Admission

| | | |
|---|---|---|
| Is the ... open on Fridays/Sundays? | هـل الـ ... مفتوح يوم الجمعة / الأحد ؟ | hæl æl...mæftūḥ yōm æl **go**maa/æl 'æḥæd |
| When does it open? | متى يفتح ؟ | mætæ **yæf**tæḥ |
| When does it close? | متى يغلق [ يقفل ] ؟ | mætæ **yog**lak |
| How much is the admission charge? | بكم الدخول ؟ | bikæm æl do**khūl** |
| Is there any reduction for students/children? | هل يوجد تخفيض للطلبة / للأطفال ؟ | hæl **yū**gæd takh**fid** lil**ta**laba/lil'atfāl |
| Have you a guide book in English? | هل عندك دليـل سياحى بالانجليزية ؟ | hæl **in**dæk dæ**līl** siy**ā**ḥi bil 'ingili**ziy**yæ |
| Can I buy a catalogue? | هل أستطيـع أن أشترى كتالوج ؟ | hæl asta**tī**' æn æsh**tæri** kætæ**lōg** |
| Do you have any postcards? | هل عندك كروت ؟ | hæl **in**dæk ko**rūt** |
| Is it all right to take pictures? | هل أستطيع التصوير ؟ | hæl æsta**tī**' æl tas**wīr** |

| | |
|---|---|
| الدخول مجانى | ADMISSION FREE |
| ممنوع التصوير | NO CAMERAS ALLOWED |

## Who—What—When?

| | | |
|---|---|---|
| What's that building? | ماهذا المبنى ؟ | mæ **hæ**zæ æl **mæb**næ |
| Who was the...? | من كان ...؟ | mæn **kæn** |
| architect | المهندس | æl mo**hæn**dis |
| artist | الفنـان | æl fæn**næn** |
| painter | الرسام | æl ræs**sæm** |
| sculptor | النحات | æl næḥ**ḥæt** |

| | | |
|---|---|---|
| Who built it? | من بناه؟ | mæn bænāēh |
| Who painted that picture? | من رسم هذه الصورة؟ | mæn **r**æsæm hāēzihi æl **s**üra |
| When did he live? | متى عاش ؟ | mætāē āēsh |
| When was it built? | متى تم البناء ؟ | mætāē **t**æmmæ æl bināē' |
| Where's the house where ... lived? | أين المنزل الذى عـاش فيه ... ؟ | æynæ æl **m**ænzil ællæzi āēshæ fih |
| We're interested in... | نحن مهتمين بـ ... | næḥno mohtæmmïn bi |
| antiques | الأنتيكـات | æl æntikæt |
| archeology | الآثـار | æl āsār |
| art | الفن | æl fæn |
| botany | النبـاتات | æl næbāētāēt |
| ceramics | الفخار | æl fokh**kh**ār |
| coins | العملات | æl 'omlāēt |
| crafts | العمل اليدوى | æl 'æmæl æl **y**ædæwi |
| fine arts | الفنون الجميلة | æl fonün æl gæmïlæ |
| folk art | الفنون الشعبية | æl fonün æl shæ'biyyæ |
| furniture | الفرش [الموبيليا] | æl færsh [æl mobilyæ] |
| geology | الجيولوجيا | æl zhiyolozhiæ |
| hieroglyphics | الهيروغليفيات | æl hiroglifiyyāēt |
| history | التـاريخ | æl tāērïkh |
| local crafts | الفنون المحلية | æl fonün æl mæḥællïyyæ |
| medicine | الطب | æl tibb |
| music | الموسيقى | æl müsïka |
| painting | الرسم | æl ræsm |
| pottery | الخزف | æl **kh**æzæf |
| prehistory | ما قبل التاريخ | māē kabl æl tāērïkh |
| sculpture | النعت | æl næḥt |
| zoology | علم الحيوان | ilm æl ḥæyæ**w**āēn |
| Where's the ... department? | أين قسم ... ؟ | æynæ kism |

78

Just the adjective you've been looking for...

| It's... | | |
|---|---|---|
| | هذا ... | hǣzæ |
| amazing | مدهش | modhish |
| awful | مخيف | mokhif |
| beautiful | جميل | gæmil |
| excellent | ممتاز | momtǣz |
| interesting | مهم | mohim |
| magnificent | عظيم | azīm |
| monumental | عظيم | azīm |
| sinister | مشئوم | mæsh'ūm |
| strange | غريب | gærīb |
| stupendous | هائل | hǣ'il |
| superb | بديع | bædi' |
| terrible | مخيف | mokhif |
| terrifying | مفزع | mofzi' |
| tremendous | هائل | hǣ'il |

## Religious services

Islam is the religion of 90 per cent of the population of the Middle East, although Lebanon is almost evenly divided between Moslems and Christians. Among the Christian denominations, the Coptic Church is the largest with over six million adherents. Eastern Orthodox and Uniate Catholic churches are also found throughout the area. Small Protestant and Jewish groups exist in many Arab cities.

The faith of nearly 700 million people, Islam is the youngest of the world's great religions. The Koran represents the written revelations of God to the prophet Mohammed, and many of its greatest precepts parallel those of the Bible. In fact, Islam acknowledges the validity of Christian and Jewish teachings.

Spread principally through North Africa, the Middle East and large parts of Asia, Islam is divided into two major bodies plus many sects. But among the basic practices which should be followed by all Moslems are prayer five times daily facing Mecca, fasting during the sacred month of Ramadan, almsgiving and at least one pilgrimage to Mecca during the lifetime of each Moslem. The Koran forbids eating pork, drinking alcohol and gambling, but just as in the Christian West, modern life is bringing about a more relaxed attitude towards the observance of these practices.

Mosques are always open to visitors, except during worship. Picture-taking is permitted. The floors of the mosques are covered with beautifully-woven prayer rugs. To avoid soiling them, visitors and worshippers alike must remove their shoes before entering. At large mosques, over-sized slippers are available to visitors. If you make use of them it's customary to give the attendant a small tip. Don't wear shorts, miniskirts or bare-shouldered blouses in the mosque, and remember not to walk in front of people who are in prayer.

| Is there a/an... near here? | هل يوجد... قريب من هنا؟ | hæl yūgæd ... karīb min honāē |
| Catholic church | كنيسة كاثوليكية | kinīsæ kætōlikiyyæ |
| Orthodox church | كنيسة أورثودوكس | kinīsæ ortodoksiyyæ |
| Protestant church | كنيسة بروتستنت | kinīsæ protistant |
| mosque | جامع | gāēmi′ |
| synagogue | معبد يهودى | mæ æbæd yæhūdi |
| At what time are the services? | ما هى مواقيت الصلاة؟ | mæ hiyæ mæwākīt æl salāh |

# Relaxing

### Cinema (movies)—Theatre

There are many open-air cinemas operating from June to September which have double- or triple-feature programmes after sundown. The conventional indoor cinema has a feature film preceded by a newsreel, a documentary and commercials.

In both Egypt and Lebanon, American and English films are very popular and are shown in their original versions. In Egypt, the first showing normally starts at 3.30 p.m. except on Sundays and Fridays when there's a matinee at 10.30 a.m.

Theatre curtain time is usually 9.30 p.m. Booking in advance is a must. You can find out what's on by consulting the newspapers or publications of the type "This Week in…"

A renowned marionette show performs at special theatres in Egypt to the delight of young and old alike.

| Have you the most recent "This Week in…"? | هل عندك آخر عدد من الأسبوع فى … ؟ | hæl ændæk āēkhir ædæd min æl 'osbū fi |
| What's on at the cinema tonight? | ما هى الأفلام مساء اليوم ؟ | mæ hiyæ æl 'æflāēm misāē' æl yōm |
| What's playing at the theatre? | ما هى المسرحيات ؟ | mæ hiyæ æl masraḥiyyāēt |
| What sort of play is it? | ما نوع المسرحية ؟ | mæ nō' æl masraḥiyya |
| Who's it by? | من المؤلف ؟ | mæn æl mo'ællif |
| Where's that new film by … playing? | أين يدور فيلم… الجديد ؟ | æynæ yædūr film…æl gædīd |

| Can you recommend (a)...? | هل تنصحنى بـ . . . ؟ | hæl tænsaḥni bi |
| good film | فيلم جيد | film gæyyid |
| comedy | كوميديا | komidyæ |
| drama | دراما | drāma |
| musical | أوبريت | obērēt |
| revue | عرض فنى | ard fænni |
| thriller | فيلم بوليسى | film bolīsi |
| Western | فيلم رعاة البقر | film roāēt æl bakar |
| I'd like to see a puppet show. | أريد أن أشاهد عرضاً للعرائس . | orīd æn oshāēhid ard lil ara'is |
| What time does it begin? | متى يبدأ ؟ | mætā yæbdæ' |
| What time does the show end? | متى ينتهى العرض ؟ | mætā yæntæhi æl 'ard |
| What time does the first evening performance start? | متى تبدأ أول حفلة فى المساء ؟ | mætā tæbdæ' æwwæl ḥæflæ fil mæsæ' |
| Are there any tickets for tonight? | هل توجد تذاكر لليلة ؟ | hæl tūgæd tæzāēkir lil lēlæ |
| I want to reserve 2 tickets for the show on Saturday evening.* | أريد أن أحجز تذكرتين لحفلة يوم السبت مساء . | orīd æn æḥgiz tazkartēn liḥæflit yōm æl sæbt mæsāē'æn |
| Can I have a ticket for the matinee on Tuesday? | أريد تذكرة للحفلة الماتينية يوم الثلاثاء . | orīd tazkara lil ḥæflæ æl mætinē yōm æl solæsāē' |
| I want a seat in the stalls (orchestra). | أريد مكاناً فى الصالة . | orīd mækāēn fil sāla |
| Not too far back. | ليس الى الوراء كثيراً . | læysæ ilāē æl warā' kæsīran |

* see grammar

82

## Opera—Ballet—Concert

Don't miss the opportunity to attend Middle Eastern music and dancing performances. At Lebanon's Baalbek ruins, ballets and concerts are held in the temple of Bacchus where local and internationally known artists perform. Among sound-and-light shows, you'll not want to miss the impressive production given at the Pyramids and the Citadel in Cairo and in Karnak.

In Beirut and Cairo you can also go to recitals and symphony concerts performed by both local and visiting artists.

| | | |
|---|---|---|
| Where's the opera house? | أين دار الأوبرا ؟ | æynæ dār æl 'obira |
| Where's the concert hall? | أين صالة الموسيقى ؟ | æynæ sālit æl mūsīka |
| What's on at the opera tonight? | ماذا فى الأوبرا مساء اليوم؟ | mǣzæ fi æl 'obira mæsǣ' æl yōm |
| Who's singing? | من يغنى ؟ | mæn yogænni |
| Who's dancing? | من يرقص ؟ | mæn yærkos |
| What time does the programme start? | متى يبدأ البرنامج ؟ | mætǣ yæbdæ' æl bir-nǣmig |
| What orchestra is playing? | ما الفرقة التى تعزف ؟ | mǣ æl firka æl læti tææzif |
| What are they playing? | ماذا يعزفون ؟ | mǣzæ yææzifūn |
| Who's the conductor? | من رئيس الفرقة ؟ | mæn ra'īs æl firka |

---

| | |
|---|---|
| آسف لا توجد أية مقاعد . | I'm sorry, we're sold out. |
| لم يبق سوى بعض المقاعد فى البلكون . | There are only a few seats in the balcony (circle). |
| أريد أن أرى تذكرتك من فضلك . | May I see your ticket? |

## Night clubs

Night clubs are pretty much the same the world over, particularly when it comes to inflated prices. For most night clubs jacket and tie are sufficient.

In Beirut, the night clubs have a decidedly French flavour. If you only visit one night club during your visit, make sure the floor show features belly-dancers.

| | | |
|---|---|---|
| Can you recommend a good night club? | هل تنصحنى بملهى ليلى جيد ؟ | hæl tansaḥni bi **mælhæ læyli gæyyid** |
| Is there a floor show? | هل يوجد عرض فنى ؟ | hæl yūgæd 'ard **fænni** |
| Are there belly-dancers? | هل توجد راقصات شرقية ؟ | hæl tūgæd rākisāt shar-kiyya |
| What time does the floor show start? | متى يبدأ العرض الفنى ؟ | mætæ yæbdæ' æl 'ard æl fænni |
| Is evening dress necessary? | هل لبس السهرة ضرورى ؟ | hæl libs æl **sahra** darūri |

## And once inside ...

| | | |
|---|---|---|
| A table for 2, please. | ترابيزة [طاولة] لـ ٢ من فضلك . | tarabēzæ [**tawl**a] li 2 min **fadl**ak |
| My name's... I booked a table for 4. | اسمى ... لقد حجزت ترابيزة [طاولة]لـ ٤ . | ismi...lakad ḥægæzt tarabēza [**tawl**a] li 4 |
| We haven't got a reservation. | ليس عندنا حجز . | læysæ indænæ ḥægz |

FOR NUMBERS, see page 175

## Dancing

| | | |
|---|---|---|
| Where can we go dancing? | أين يمكن الذهاب للرقص ؟ | æynæ **yom**kin æl zih**ǣb** lil raks |
| Is there a discotheque anywhere here? | هل توجد مراقص هنا ؟ | hæl t**ū**gæd mar**ā**kis hon**ā** |
| There's a ball at the... | هناك حفلة فى ... | hon**ā**k ḥæflæ fi |
| Would you like to dance? | هل ترقصين ؟ | hæl tærko**sī**n |
| May I have this dance? | هـــل تسمحى لى بهذه الرقصة ؟ | hæl tæsmaḥi li bih**ǣ**zihi æl **raks**a |

## Do you happen to play ... ?

On rainy days, this page may solve your problems.

| | | |
|---|---|---|
| Do you happen to play chess? | هل تلعب الشطرنج ؟ | hæl tæl'æb shata**rang** |
| I'm afraid I don't. | آسف لا ألعب . | **ā**sif l**ǣ** 'æl'æb |
| No, but I'll give you a game of back-gammon/domino. | لا . ولكنى أستطيع أن ألعب الطاولة / الدومينو . | l**ǣ** wæ læ**kin**ni astat**ī** æn 'ǣl'æb æl **taw**la/æl domino |
| king | ملك | **mæ**lik |
| queen | وزير | wæz**ī**r |
| castle (rook) | طابية | **tab**ya |
| bishop | فيـــل | fil |
| knight | حصان [فرس] | ḥos**ā**n [far**as**] |
| pawn | عسكرى [بيدق] | **æs**kæri [b**ē**dæ'] |
| Check mate! | كش مات ! | kishsh m**ā**t |
| Do you play cards? | هل تلعب ورق [كوتشينة] ؟ | hæl tæl'æb **wæ**ræk [kot**shī**næ] |
| ace | آس | **ā**s |
| king | شايب [روا] | sh**ǣ**yib [rw**ā**] |
| queen | بنت | bint |
| jack | ولد | **wæ**læd |
| joker | جوكر | **zhō**kar |

| spades | بستونى | bæstōni |
| hearts | كوبا | kobba |
| diamonds | دينارى | dināēri |
| clubs | سباتى | sobāēti |

Though gambling is forbidden by the Koran, casinos are operated all-year round in the Middle East for free-spending foreigners. To enter a casino, you must be over 21 and show your passport. When in Lebanon, visit the *Casino du Liban*, claimed to rival the casino of Monte Carlo. Lebanon's casino palace is found 13 miles from Beirut at Maalmeltein.

## Oriental chess

In the Middle East, a very popular game is oriental chess, or backgammon, called *tawla* in Arabic. Shown below is the backgammon board. The game is played with dice. The winner is he who first has all his counters on his side.

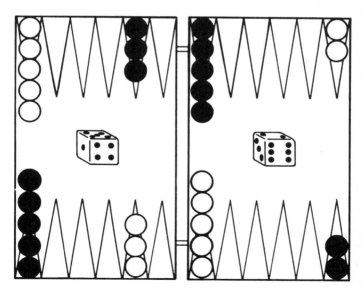

86

## Sport

Football (soccer) is probably the favourite sport in the Middle East, especially in Egypt, but basketball, tennis and water sports are also very popular. Given the temperate-to-hot climate, water sports are practiced enthusiastically on the Mediterranean coastlines of Egypt and Lebanon and on the Nile. There is horse-racing on Saturdays and Sundays in Egypt.

| | | |
|---|---|---|
| Where's the nearest golf course? | أين أقرب ملعب جولف ؟ | æynæ akrab mæl'æb golf |
| Can we hire (rent) clubs? | هل يمكن تأجير العصيان ؟ | hæl yomkin tæ'gīr æl 'osyān |
| Where are the tennis courts? | أين ملاعب التنس ؟ | æynæ mælāè'ib æl tinis |
| Can I hire rackets? | هل يمكن تأجير المضارب ؟ | hæl yomkin tæ'gīr æl madārib |
| What's the charge per...? | ما الثمن لمدة ... ؟ | mā æl tæmæn limoddæt |
| day/round/hour | يوم / لفة / ساعة | yōm/læffæ/sāè'æ |
| What's the admission charge? | بكم الدخول ؟ | bikæm æl dokhūl |
| Is there a swimming pool here? | هل يوجد حمام سباحة [بيسين] هنا ؟ | hæl yūgæd ḥæmmāem sibāèḥæ [pisīn] honæ |
| Is it open-air or indoors? | هل هو مكشوف أم مغطى ؟ | hæl howæ mækshūf æm mogattā |
| Is it heated? | هل هو مدفأ ؟ | hæl howæa modæffæ' |
| Can one swim in the lake/river? | هل يمكن الاستحمام فى البحيرة / النهر ؟ | hæl yomkin æl 'istiḥmāem fil boḥæyra/æl nahr |
| I'd like to see a boxing/wrestling match. | أريد مشاهدة مباراة ملاكمة / مصارعة . | orīd moshāèhædæt mobārāt molækmæ/ mosar'a |
| Can you get me 2 tickets?* | هل يمكنك شراء تذكرتين لى ؟ | hæl yomkinæk shirā' tæzkartēn li |

* see grammar

| | | |
|---|---|---|
| Is there a football (soccer) match any-where this Friday? | هل توجد مباراة كرة قدم يوم الجمعة ؟ | hæl **tūg**æd mubarāt **k**orit **k**adam yōm æl **g**omaa |
| Who's playing? | من يلعب ؟ | mæn yæl'æb |
| Is there any good fishing around here? | هل الصيد جيد هنا ؟ | hæl æl sēd gæyyid honāe |
| Do I need a permit? | هل أنا محتاج لترخيص ؟ | hæl ænāe moḥtāeg litarkhīs |
| Where can I get one? | أين يمكن الحصول على ترخيص ؟ | æynæ yomkin æl ḥosūl ælāe tarkhis |
| Is there a bowling alley/billiard hall near here? | هل يوجد ملعب بولنج / بلياردو قريب ؟ | hæl **y**ūgæd **m**æl'æb **b**ōling/bilyardo karīb |

## On the beach

| | | |
|---|---|---|
| Where's the beach? | أين الشاطىء ؟ | æynæ æl **sh**āti' |
| Is it safe for swimming? | هل الاستحمام أمان ؟ | hæl æl 'istiḥ**māe**m 'æ**māe**n |
| Is there a lifeguard? | هل يوجد غطاس ؟ | hæl **y**ūgæd gattās |
| Is it safe for children? | هل هو أمان للأطفال ؟ | hæl howæ 'æmān lil'atfāl |
| It's very calm. | انه هادىء جداً . | innæho **h**āedi' giddæn |
| Is it a good place for snorkelling? | هل هو مكـان مناسب للغطس ؟ | hæl howæ mækāen monāesib lil gats |
| Are there dangerous currents? | هل توجد تيارات خطيرة ؟ | hæl **t**ūgæd tayyārāt khatīra |
| What time is high/low tide? | متى المـد / الجزر ؟ | mætæ æl mædd/æl gæzr |
| What's the tempera-ture of the water? | ما درجة حرارة المياه ؟ | mæ **d**aragit ḥarārit æl miy**āe**h |
| I want to hire a/an/some... | أريد تأجير ... | orīd tæ'**gīr** |
| air mattress | مرتبة هواء | **m**ærtæbit hæ**w**æ' |
| bathing hut | كابينة لخلع الملابس | kabīnæ likhæl'il mælāebis |
| bathing suit | مايوه | mæyō |

88

| deck chair | كرسى بلاج قماش | **kor**si plǣzh 'om**ǣsh** |
| skin-diving equipment | أدوات غطس | ædæw**ǣt** gats |
| sunshade | شمسية | shæm**siyyæ** |
| swimming belt | حزام نجاة [عوامة] | ḥizǣm nægǣ (æww**ǣ**mæ) |
| tent | خيمـة | kh**ē**mæ |
| water skis | أدوات انزلاق على الماء | ædæw**ǣt** inzil**ǣk** 'ælǣ æl mǣ' |
| Where can I rent a...? | أين أستأجر ... ؟ | æynæ æstæ'gir |
| canoe | مركب | **mæ**rkib |
| motor boat | مركب بموتور [لنش] | **mæ**rkib bimot**ōr** [lænsh] |
| rowing boat | مركب بمقاديف | **mæ**rkib bi mæ'**ǣdīf** |
| sailing boat | مركب شراعية | **mæ**rkib shira'**iyyæ** |
| What's the charge per hour? | بكم الساعة ؟ | bikæm æl s**ǣ**'æ |

| شاطىء خاص | ممنوع الاستعمام |
| PRIVATE BEACH | NO BATHING |

## Winter sports

From about mid-December until about mid-May you can
ski at several locations in Lebanon.

| I want to hire a/ some... | أريد استئجار ... | or**īd** isti'gār |
| ski boots | بوط سكى | b**ōt** ski |
| ski poles | عصى سكى | as**ā** ski |
| skiing equipment | معدات سكى | mo'id**dǣt** ski |
| skis | سكى | sk**ī** |
| toboggan | زحليقة | zoḥl**ē**'æ |

# Camping—Countryside

A sunny climate makes camping possible all year round—particularly along the Mediterranean Coast. However, campsites and facilities are limited, so check with the tourist office before setting out on your own. You can also camp near a house or on private land, but get permission from the owner first. People will always be happy to help you, and if you're lucky they'll even invite you in to share their meal.

| Can we camp here? | هل نستطيع أن نعسكر هنا ؟ | hæl næstatī æn no'æskir honǣ |
| Where can one camp for the night? | أين نستطيع أن نعسكر الليلة ؟ | æynæ nastatī æn no'æskir æl lēlæ |
| Is there a camping site near here? | هل يوجد معسكر قريب من هنا ؟ | hæl yūgæd mo'askar karīb min honǣ |
| Is there drinking water? | هل توجد مياه للشرب ؟ | hæl tūgæd miyǣh lil shorb |
| Are there shopping facilities on the site? | هل يوجد دكان فى المعسكر ؟ | hæl yūgæd dokkǣn fil mo'askar |
| Are there showers/ toilets? | هل يوجد دش / حمام ؟ | hæl yūgæd doshsh/ ḥæmmǣm |
| What's the charge per day...? | بكم الليلة ... ؟ | bikæm æl lēlæ |
| per person | لشخص | lishakhs |
| for a car | لسيارة | lisæyyāra |
| for a tent | لخيمة | likhēmæ |
| Is there a youth hostel anywhere near here? | هل يوجد بيت شباب قريب ؟ | hæl yūgæd bēt shæbǣb karīb |
| Do you know anyone who can put us up for the night? | هل تعرف أحدا يقبل أن يسكننا عنده الليلة ؟ | hæl taarif æhædæn yakbæl æn yosækkinonæ indæho æl lēlæ |

FOR CAMPING EQUIPMENT, see page 107

ممنوع التخييم

CAMPING PROHIBITED

| How far is it to...? | ما هى المسافة الى ... ؟ | mæ hiyæ æl mæsæfæ ilæ |
| How far is the next village? | ما هى المسافة الى القرية القادمة ؟ | mæ hiyæ æl mæsæfæ ilæ æl **kar**ya æl kādimæ |
| Are we on the right road for...? | هل نحن على الطريق الصحيح الى ... ؟ | hæl næḥno ælæ æl tarīk æl saḥīḥ ilæ |
| Where does this road lead to? | الى أين يؤدى هذا الطريق ؟ | ilæ æynæ yo'æddi hæzæ æl tarīk |
| Can you show us on the map where we are? | أين نحن على الغريطة من فضلك ؟ | æynæ næḥno ælæ æl kharita min **fad**lak |

## Landmarks

| airfield | مطار | matār |
| bridge | كوبرى [جسر] | **kob**ri [zhisr] |
| building | مبنى | mæbnæ |
| canal | قناة | kanæ |
| castle | قصر | kasr |
| cliff | حافة الجبل | ḥæffit æl gæbæl |
| copse | أعشاب | ææshæb |
| crossroads | مفترق طرق [تقاطع] | **mof**tarak **to**rok [takāto] |
| desert | صحراء | saḥrā' |
| excavations | تنقيب عن الآثار | tankīb æn æl āsār |
| farm | عزبة | '**iz**ba |
| ferry | معدية | mi'æd**diy**yæ |
| field | حقـل | ḥakl |
| footpath | سكة | **sik**kæ |
| hamlet | قرية | **kar**ya |
| hill | تـل | tæll |
| house | بيت | bēt |

| inn | استراحة | istirāḥa |
| lake | بحيرة | boḥēra |
| mound | تـل | tæll |
| mountain | جبل | gæbæl |
| mountain range | سلسلة جبال | silsilit gibāl |
| oasis | واحة | wāēḥæ |
| path | سكة | sikkæ |
| plain | سهل | sæhl |
| plantation | مزرعة | mazraa |
| pool | بركة | birkæ |
| railway | خط سكة حديد | khatt sikkæ ḥædīd |
| river | نهر | nahr |
| road | طريق | tarīk |
| ruins | أطلال | atlāl |
| sand dunes | تلال رملية | tilāēl ramliyyæ |
| sea | بحر | baḥr |
| spring | منبع | mænbææ |
| tower | برج | borg |
| track | سكة | sikkæ |
| tree | شجرة | shagara |
| valley | وادى | wāēdi |
| village | قرية | karya |
| wadi | وادى | wāēdi |
| well | بئر | biʾr |
| wood | غابة | gāēbæ |

| What's the name of this place? | ما اسم هذا المكان ؟ | mæ ism hāēzæ æl mækāēn |
| How high is that mountain? | ما ارتفاع هذا الجبل ؟ | mæ irtifāēʿ hāēzæ æl gæbæl |

...and if you're tired of walking, you can always try hitchhiking—though you may have to wait a long time for a lift.

| Can you give me a lift to...? | من فضلك وصلنى الى ... | min fadlak wassalni ilāē |

# Making friends

## Introductions

Despite the language barrier, you'll have no problem in striking up a conversation with Arabs, especially when they realize that you're a foreigner. As a matter of fact, they'll probably start the conversation first. Arabs are eager to help foreigners, and they're curious to learn about your country and way of life. It's quite possible that a chance meeting with an Arab will soon lead to an invitation to meet his family at home. Do accept, as such spontaneous hospitality is sincere, and bring some sweets or flowers for the hostess.

Here are a few phrases to get you started.

| How do you do? How are you? | ازيك [كيفك] ؟ | izzæyyæk [kifæk] |
| Very well, thank you. | بخير . الحمد لله . | bikhēr. ælḥæmdolillǣh |
| How's life? | كيف الحال ؟ | kæyfæl ḥǣl |
| Fine thanks. And you? | كويس شكراً . وأنت ؟ | kwæyyis shokran. wæ intæ |
| May I introduce Miss... | أقدم لك الآنسة ... | okaddim læk æl 'ǣnissæ |
| I'd like you to meet a friend of mine. | أحب أن تقابل صديقاً لى . | oḥib æn tokābil sadīkan li |
| Ali, this is... | يا على ، هذا ... | yǣ ali hǣzæ |
| My name's... | اسمى ... | ismi |
| Glad to know you. | تشرفنا . | tæsharrafna |

## Follow-up

| How long have you been here? | منذ متى وأنت هنا ؟ | monzo mætǣ wæ intæ hobǣ |
| We've been here a week. | نحن هنا منذ أسبوع . | næḥno honǣ monzo osbū |

| Is this your first visit? | هل هذه أول زيارة لك ؟ | hæl hǣzihi **awwal** ziyāra lǣk |
|---|---|---|
| No, we came here last year. | لا . أتينا السنة الماضية . | lǣ. ætæynæ æl sænæ æl mādiyæ |
| Are you enjoying your stay? | هل أنت مبسوط هنا ؟ | hæl 'æntæ mabsūt honæ |
| Yes. I like ... very much. | نعم ... تعجبني جداً . | næ'æm ... to'giboni giddæn |
| Are you on your own? | هل أنت وحدك ؟ | hæl æntæ **wæ**ḥdæk |
| I'm with... | أنا مع ... | ænǣ mæææ |
| my wife | زوجتى | zæwgæti |
| my husband | زوجى | zæwgi |
| my family | أسرتى | osrati |
| my parents | والداى | wǣlidǣy |
| some friends | أصحابى | 'ashābi |
| Where do you come from? | من أين تأتى ؟ | min æynæ tæ'ti |
| What part of ... do you come from? | من أى مكان فى ... تأتى ؟ | min ayy mækǣn fi ... tæ'ti |
| I'm from... | أنا من ... | ænǣ min |
| Where are you staying? | أين تسكن ؟ | æynæ tæskon |
| I'm a student. | أنا طالب . | ænǣ tālib |
| What are you studying? | ماذا تدرس ؟ | mǣzæ tædross |
| We're here on holiday. | نحن هنا فى اجازة [فرصة] . | næḥno honæ fi ægǣzæ [forsa] |
| I'm here on a business trip. | أنا هنا لشغل . | ænǣ honæ li shogl |
| What kind of business are you in? | ما ذا تشتغل ؟ | mǣzæ tæshtægil |
| I hope we'll see you again soon. | أرجو أن أراك مرة أخرى قريباً ان شاء الله . | argū æn arākæ **marra** okhrā karībæn 'in shǣ'allāh |
| See you later/See you tomorrow. | الى اللقاء / أراك غداً . | ilǣ æl likā'/arākæ gædæn |

94

## The weather

The Arabs don't talk about the weather as much as we do, but if you can't think of a better way to enter into conversation with someone, try...

| What a lovely day! | انه يوم جميل . | innæho yōm gæ**mil** |
| What awful weather! | الجو سيء [وحش] . | æl gæw **sæyyi´** [**wiḥish**] |
| Isn't it hot/cold today? | أليس الجو حاراً / بارداً اليوم ؟ | ælæysæ æl gæw ḥarr/bærd æl yōm |
| The wind is very strong. | الهواء شديد جداً . | æl hæ**wāē´** shædīd **gidd**æn |
| What's the temperature outside? | ما درجة الحرارة بالخارج ؟ | mæ **dara**git æl ḥarāra bil **khāē**rig |
| What's the weather forecast? | ما هى التنبؤات الجوية ؟ | mæ hiyæ æl tænæbbo´**āē**t æl gæw**wiyyæ** |

## Invitations

| My wife and I would like you to dine with us on... | زوجتى وأنا نحب أن تتعشى معنا يوم ... | zæwgæti wæ ænāē noḥibb æn tætæ´**æsh**shāē **mæ**´æ-næ yōm |
| Can you come to dinner tomorrow night? | هل تستطيع أن تأتى للعشاء مساء الغد ؟ | hæl tastatī æn **tæ**´ti lil æsh**āē**´ mæs**āē**´ æl gædd |
| Can you join us for a drink this evening? | هل تشاركنا فى مشروب مساء اليوم ؟ | hæl tushāē**rik**næ fi mashrūb mæs**āē**´ æl yōm |
| There's a party. Are you coming? | هناك حفلة هل تأتى ؟ | hon**āē**k ḥæflæ. hæl **tæ**´ti |
| That's very kind of you. | هذا لطيف جداً منك . | h**āē**zæ latīf **gidd**æn min**kæ** |
| Great, I'd love to come. | عظيم ، يسرنى أن أحضر . | a**zim**. yæsor**ro**ni æn aḥdar |

| What time shall we come? | متى نأتى ؟ | mætā næ'ti |
| May I bring a friend (male/female)? | هل يمكن أن يأتى صديقى / صديقتى ؟ | hæl **yom**kin æn yæ'ti sadiki/sadikati |
| I'm afraid we've got to go now. | نستأذن فى الرحيل . | næstæ'zin fil raḥil |
| Next time you must come to visit us. | المرة القادمة يجب أن تـأتى لزيارتنا . | æl **marra** æl kādimæ **yæ**gib æn tæ'ti liziyāratinæ |
| Thank you very much for an enjoyable evening. | شكراً جزيلا على هذه السهرة الجميلة . | **shok**ran gæzīlæn 'ælæ hāzihi æl **sah**ra æl gæmīlæ |
| Thanks for the party. It was great. | شكراً على الحفلة . كانت عظيمة . | **shok**ran 'ælā æl ḥæflæ. kānæt azima |

## Dating

| Would you like a cigarette? | سيجارة ؟ | sigāra |
| Have you got a light, please? | أريد أن أولّـع من فضلك. | orid æn awællæ min **fad**lak |
| Can I get you a drink? | هل أقدم لك كأساً ؟ | hæl o**kad**dim læki kæ'sæn |
| Excuse me, could you please help me? | هل تساعدينى من فضلك ؟ | hæl tosæ'i**di**ni min **fad**lik |
| I'm lost. Can you show me the way to...? | أنا تائه . من فضلك أرشدينى الى . . . | ænā tā'ih. min **fad**lik ærshi**di**ni ilā |
| Are you waiting for someone? | هل تنتظرين أحداً ؟ | hæl tantazi**ri**næ æ**ḥæ**dæn |
| Are you free this evening? | هل أنت فاضية مساء اليوم ؟ | hæl **æn**ti **fad**yā mæsā' æl yōm |
| Would you like to go out with me tonight? | هل تحبين الخروج معى الليلة ؟ | hæl to**ḥib**binæ æl kho**rūg** mæ'i æl **lē**læ |

| Would you like to go dancing? | هل تحبين الذهاب للرقص ؟ | hæl toḥibbīnæ æl zihæb lil raks |
| I know a good discotheque/restaurant. | أعرف مرقصاً/مطعماً جيداً . | æ'ærif **mark**as/**mat**'am **gæ**yyid |
| Shall we go to the cinema (movies)? | هل نذهب الى السينما ؟ | hæl **næz**hæb ilæ æl sinimæ |
| I'd love to, thank you. | نعم أحب ، شكراً . | næææm oḥibb **shok**ran |
| Where shall we meet? | أين نتقابل ؟ | æynæ nætæ**kā**bæl |
| When shall I pick you up? | في أى ساعة أمر عليك للخروج ؟ | fi æyy **sā**'æ æmorr ælæyki lil khorūg |
| I'll call for you at 8. | سأحضر الساعة ٨ . | sæ'aḥdar æl **sā**'æ 8 |
| May I take you home? | هل أوصلك الى منزلك ؟ | hæl awas**sa**lik ilæ mænzilik |
| Can I see you again tomorrow? | هل نتقابل غداً ؟ | hæl nætæ**kā**bæl **gæ**dæn |
| Thank you, it's been a wonderful evening. | شكراً . كانت سهرة ممتازة . | **shok**ran. **kæ**næt **sah**ra mom**tæ**zæ |
| I've enjoyed myself tremendously. | أنا انبسطت جداً . | 'ænæ inba**satt gid**dæn |
| What's your telephone number? | ما نمرة تليفونك ؟ | mæ **nim**rit tilifōnik |
| Do you live with your family? | هل تسكنين مع أسرتك ؟ | hæl tæsko**nī**næ mæ'æ osratik |
| Do you live alone? | هل تسكنين وحدك ؟ | hæl tæsko**nī**næ **wæ**ḥdik |
| What time do you have to be back? | متى يجب أن تعودى الى المنزل ؟ | mætæ **yæ**gib 'æn tæ'ūdi ilæ æl **mæ**nzil |

# Shopping guide

This shopping guide is designed to help you find what you want with ease, accuracy and speed. It features:

1. a list of all major shops, stores and services;
2. some general expressions required when shopping to allow you to be specific and selective;
3. full details of the shops and services most likely to concern you. Here you will find advice, alphabetical lists of items and conversion charts listed under the headings below.

## Advice

In Egypt and Jordan, stores are open from 8.30 a.m. to 12.30 p.m. and from 4 to 7 p.m., Monday to Thursday, and from 8.30 a.m. to 12.30 p.m. on Saturdays. Although some small shops remain open on Friday, offices and department stores are closed. On Sunday the large stores are shut, but all other activities continue normally. In Lebanon, hours vary according to the season: from November to May stores are open from 8.30 a.m. to 1 p.m. and from 3 to 6 p.m., Monday to Friday, and from 8.30 a.m. until 12.30 p.m. on Saturdays. During the summer months they're open on weekdays from 8 a.m. until 1 p.m. only and are closed on Saturdays and Sundays.

*Souk* means "market" in Arabic. It's composed of a maze of narrow, winding alleys where all kinds of tradesmen and artisans are grouped together.

In the *souk* you'll see all sorts of jewellers and artisans at work inlaying wood with enamel and ivory, engraving or hammering copper or making pottery. Antique dealers abound, and merchants sell fine rugs and brocades—all this in an atmosphere scented with sandalwood, cinnamon and musk.

If you are interested in antiques, with a little luck you might come across an ancient coin, a piece of Coptic cloth or a statuette dating back to the pharaohs. Be sure to demand a museum certificate guaranteeing the authenticity of any very old objects you buy.

Remember that selling and bargaining are Eastern customs not without a certain charm. As you browse through the *souk*, take your time, and don't hesitate to accept a cup of coffee or mint tea offered you by a merchant.

## Shops, stores and services

| | | |
|---|---|---|
| Where's the nearest...? | أين أقرب ... ؟ | æynæ akrab |
| antique shop | محل أنتيكات | mæḥæll æntikāt |
| art gallery | معرض فنون | maarad fonūn |
| bakery | مخبز | mækhbæz |
| bank | بنك | bænk |
| barber's | حلاق | ḥællāk |
| bazaar | بازار [سوق] | bazār [sūk] |
| beauty salon | صالون تجميل | salōn tægmil |
| bookshop | مكتبة | mæktæbæ |
| butcher | جزار [لحام] | gazzār [læḥḥām] |
| candy store | محل حلويات [ملبّس] | mæḥæll ḥælæwiyyāt [milæbbiss] |
| chemist's | أجزخانة [فرماشية] | ægzækhānæ [færmæshiyyæ] |
| clothing store | محل ملابس | mæḥæll mælābis |
| cobbler | جزمجى [كندرجى] | gæzmægi [kindarzhi] |
| dairy | محل ألبان | mæḥill ælbān |
| dentist | طبيب أسنان | tabib æsnān |
| department store | محل كبير | mæḥæll kæbir |
| doctor | دكتور | doktōr |
| dressmaker | خياطة | khayyāta |
| drugstore | أجزخانة [فرماشية] | ægzækhānæ [færmæshiyyæ] |
| dry cleaner | محل تنظيف ملابس | mæḥæll tanzif mælābis |
| fishmonger | محل سمك | mæḥæll sæmækk |
| florist | محل زهور | mæḥæll zohūr |
| furrier | محل فرو | mæḥæll farrw |
| greengrocer | خضرى | khodari |
| grocery | بقال | bakkāl |
| hairdresser's (ladies) | صالون تجميل | salōn tægmil |
| hardware store | محل أدوات منزلية | mæḥæll ædæwāt mænziliyyæ |
| hat shop | محل برانيط | mæḥæll baranit |

| | | |
|---|---|---|
| hospital | مستشفى | mostæshfæ |
| ironmonger | محل أدوات منزلية | mæḥæll ædæw**āt** mænzili**yy**æ |
| jeweller | جواهرجى | gæwæ**hi**rgi |
| laundry | غسيل ومكوة | gæs**il** wæ mækwæ |
| leather-goods store | محل مصنوعات جلدية | mæḥæll masnū'**āt** gil**di**yyæ |
| market | سوق | sūk |
| milliner | صانعة برانيط | sāni'æt baran**it** |
| newsagent | بائع جرائد | bæ'i' garā'id |
| newsstand | كشك جرائد | koshk garā' id |
| optician | محل نظارات [عوينات] | mæḥæll nazzar**āt** [owæyn**āt**] |
| pastry shop | حلوانى | ḥælæw**ā**ni |
| perfumery | محل عطور | mæḥæll otūr |
| photographer | مصور | mosa**w**wir |
| photo shop | محل تصوير | mæḥæll taswīr |
| police station | قسم بوليس | kism bol**is** |
| post office | مكتب بريد | **mæ**ktæb bær**id** |
| shoemaker (repairs) | جزمجى [كندرجى] | gæzmægi [kind**ar**zhi] |
| shoe shop | محل جزم [أحذية] | mæḥæll gizæm [æḥziyæ] |
| souvenir shop | محل سوفنير | mæḥæll sūvin**ir** |
| sporting goods shop | محل أدوات رياضية | mæḥæll ædæw**āt** riyāddi**yy**a |
| stationer | مكتبة | **mæ**ktæbæ |
| supermarket | سوبر ماركت | **sū**pir **ma**rkit |
| sweet shop | محل حلويات [ملبس] | mæḥæll ḥælæwiyy**āt** [mil**æb**bis] |
| tailor | ترزى [خياط] | tærzi [khayy**āt**] |
| tobacconist | محل سجاير [دخان] | mæḥæll sægæ**ā**yir [dokh**khā**n] |
| travel agent | مكتب سياحى | **mæ**ktæb siyæ**ḥ**i |
| vegetable store | خضرى | **kho**dari |
| veterinarian | طبيب بيطرى | tab**ib** bitari |
| watchmaker | محل ساعات | mæḥæll sæ**ā**t |

## General expressions

Here are some expressions which will be useful to you when you're out shopping.

### Where?

| | | |
|---|---|---|
| Where's a good...? | أين يوجد ... جيد ؟ | æynæ yūgæd...gæyyid |
| Where can I find a...? | أين أجد ... ؟ | æynæ ægid |
| Where do they sell...? | أين يباع ... ؟ | æynæ yobāᵃ' |
| Can you recommend an inexpensive...? | هل يمكنك أن تنصحني بـ... رخيص ؟ | hæl yomkinæk æn tænsaḥni bi...rakhīs |
| Where's the main shopping area? | أين مركز المحلات الرئيسي ؟ | æynæ mærkæz æl mæḥillāt æl ra'īssi |
| How far is it from here? | ما بعده عن هنا ؟ | mā bo'doh æn honā |
| How do I get there? | كيف أصل اليه ؟ | kæyfæ asil ilæyhi |

### Service

| | | |
|---|---|---|
| Can you help me? | هل يمكنك مساعدتي ؟ | hæl yomkinæk mosæᵃ'ædæti |
| I'm just looking around. | انني أتفرج فقط . | innæni ætæfarrag fakatt |
| I want... | أريد ... | orīd |
| Can you show me some...? | هل يمكنك أن تريني ... ؟ | hæl yomkinæk æn torīni |
| Have you any...? | هل عندك ... ؟ | hæl indæk |

### That one

| | | |
|---|---|---|
| Can you show me that one? | من فضلك أريني هذا . | min fadlak ærīni hāzæ |
| It's over there. | انه هناك . | innæho honāk |

## Defining the article

| I want a ... one. | ... أريد شيئاً | orīd shæy'æn |
|---|---|---|
| big | كبير | kæbir |
| coloured | ملون | molæwwæn |
| dark | غامق | gāmik |
| good | جيد | gæyyid |
| heavy | ثقيل | ti'īl |
| large | كبير | kæbir |
| light (weight) | خفيف | khæfif |
| light (colour) | فاتح | fātiḥ |
| long | طويل | tawil |
| round | مستدير | mostædir |
| short | قصير | kasir |
| small | صغير | sagir |
| square | مربع | morabbaa |

| I don't want anything too expensive. | لا أريد شيئاً غاليا . | læ orīd shæy'æn gāliyæn |
|---|---|---|

## Preference

| Can you show me some more? | أريد أن أرى شيئاً آخراً من فضلك . | orīd æn arā shæy'æn ākhar min fadlak |
|---|---|---|
| Haven't you anything...? | هل عندك شيء ... ؟ | hæl indæk shē' |
| cheaper/better | أرخص / أحسن | arkhas / æḥsæn |
| larger/smaller | أكبر / أصغر | akbar / asgar |

## How much?

| How much is this? | بكم هذا ؟ | bikæm hāzæ |
|---|---|---|
| I don't understand. Please write it down. | لا أفهم . من فضلك أكتب لى الثمن . | læ æfhæm. min fadlak iktib li æl tæmæn |
| I don't want to spend more than... | لا أريد أن أدفع أكثر من ... | læ orīd æn ædfææ aktar min |

FOR NUMBERS, see page 175

## Decision

| | | |
|---|---|---|
| That's just what I want. | هذا هو المطلوب . | hæzæ howæl matlūb |
| No, I don't like it. | لا . لا تعجبني . | læ. læ to'giboni |
| I'll take it. | سآخذها . | sæ'ækhodhæ |

## Ordering

| | | |
|---|---|---|
| Can you order it for me? | هـل يمكنك أن توصى عليها لى ؟ | hæl yomkinæk æn towassi ælæyhæ li |
| How long will it take? | متى تكون جاهزة ؟ | mætæ tækūn gæhizæ |

## Delivery

| | | |
|---|---|---|
| I'll take it with me. | سآخذها معى . | sæ'ækhodhæ mæ'i |
| Deliver it to the ... hotel. | وصلها الى فندق ... | wassilhæ ilæ fondok |
| Please send it to this address. | من فضلك أرسلها الى هذا العنوان . | min fadlak ærsilhæ ilæ hæzæl 'inwæn |
| Will I have any difficulty with the customs? | هل سأجد صعوبة فى الجمرك؟ | hæl sæ'ægid so'ūba fil gomrok |

## Paying

| | | |
|---|---|---|
| How much is it? | بكم ؟ | bikæm |
| Can I pay by traveller's cheque? | هل يمكن الدفع بشيكات سياحية ؟ | hæl yomkin æl dæf' bishēkæt siyæḥiyyæ |
| Do you accept dollars/ pounds/credit cards? | هل تقبـل الدولارات / الجنيهات / بطاقات الرصيد ؟ | hæl takbal æl dōlārāt/ æl gonæyhæt/bitākāt æl rasīd |
| Haven't you made a mistake in the bill? | ألا توجد غلطة فى الفاتورة ؟ | 'ælæ tūgæd galta fil fatūra |
| Can I have a receipt, please? | أريد فاتورة [ ايصال ] من فضلك . | orīd fatūra ['isāl] min fadlak |

## Anything else?

| | | |
|---|---|---|
| No, thanks, that's all. | لا ، شكراً . يكفى هذا . | læ **shok**ran. **yæk**fi **hæ**zæ |
| Yes, I want... | نعم ، أريد ... | **næ**æm. o**rīd** |
| Thank you. Good-bye. | شكراً . مع السلامة . | **shok**ran. maassælæmæ |

## Dissatisfied

| | | |
|---|---|---|
| Can you please exchange this? | هل يمكنك تغيير هذا من فضلك ؟ | hæl yomkinæk tæ**gyir hæ**zæ min **fad**lak |
| I want to return this. | أريد ارجاع هذا . | o**rīd** ir**gæ**' **hæ**zæ |
| I'd like a refund. | أريد استرداد الثمن . | o**rīd** istir**dæd** æl **tæ**mæn |
| Here's the receipt. | هذا هو الايصال . | **hæ**zæ **how**æl 'i**sāl** |

---

| | |
|---|---|
| هل استطيع مساعدتك ؟ | Can I help you? |
| أى ... تريد ؟ | What ... would you like? |
| لون / شكل | colour/shape |
| نوع / كمية | quality/quantity |
| آسف . ليس عندى منه . | I'm sorry, we haven't any. |
| لقد انتهى ما كان عندنا منه. | We're out of stock. |
| هل نوصى لك عليه ؟ | Shall we order it for you? |
| هل تأخذه معك أم يجب أن نرسله لك ؟ | Will you take it with you or shall we send it? |
| أى شىء آخر ؟ | Anything else? |
| ... (الثمن) من فضلك . | That's ... please. |
| لا نقبل ... | We don't accept... |
| بطاقات الرصيد | credit cards |
| الشيكات السياحية | traveller's cheques |
| الشيكات الخاصة | personal cheques |

## Bookshop—Stationer's—Newsstand

In the Middle East, bookshops and stationers may be combined or separate. Newspapers and magazines may be sold in bookshops, in kiosks or at the stationer's.

| Where's the nearest...? | أين أقرب ... ؟ | æynæ akrab |
|---|---|---|
| bookshop | مكتبة | mæktæbæ |
| stationer's | محل أدوات كتابة | mæḥæll ædæwāet kitāebæ |
| newsstand | كشك جرائد | koshk garā'id |
| I want to buy a/an/some... | أريد شراء ... | orīd shirā' |
| address book | دفتر عناوين | daftar ænæwīn |
| ball-point pen | قلم حبر جاف | kalam ḥibr gāef |
| book | كتاب | kitāeb |
| box of paints | علبة ألوان | ilbit ælwāen |
| carbon paper | ورق كربون | warak karbōn |
| cellophane tape | شريط لاصق | shirīt lāsik |
| crayons | أقلام ألوان | aklām ælwāen |
| dictionary | قاموس | kamūs |
| Arabic—English | عربى — انجليزى | arabi-ingilīzi |
| English—Arabic | انجليزى — عربى | ingilīsi-arabi |
| pocket dictionary | قاموس للجيب | kamūs lil gēb |
| drawing paper | ورق رسم | warak ræsm |
| drawing pins | دبابيس رسم | dæbæbīs ræsm |
| envelopes | ظروف | zorūf |
| eraser | أستيكة [ممحاة] | æstīkæ [mimḥāeh] |
| fountain pen | قلم حبر | kalam ḥibr |
| glue | صمغ | samg |
| grammar book | كتاب نحو | kitāeb næḥw |
| guide book | دليل سياحى | dælīl siyāeḥi |
| ink | حبر | ḥibr |
| black/red/blue | أسود/أحمر/أزرق | æswæd/aḥmar/æzrak |

| labels | بطاقات | bitākāt |
|---|---|---|
| magazine | مجلة | mægællæ |
| map | خريطة | kharīta |
| map of the town | خريطة للمدينة | kharīta lil mædīnæ |
| road map | خريطة للطرق | kharīta lil **t**orok |
| newspaper | جريدة | gærīdæ |
| American/English | أمريكانى / انجليزى | æmrikāēni / ingilīzi |
| notebook | مفكرة [بلوك نوت] | mofækkira [blok-nōt] |
| note paper | ورق خطابات | warak khitabāt |
| paperback | كتاب جيب | kitāēb gēb |
| paper napkins | فوط ورق | fowatt warak |
| pen | قلم حبر | kalam ḥibr |
| pencil | قلم رصاص | kalam rosās |
| pencil sharpener | برّاية | bærrāēyæ |
| playing cards | ورق لعب [كوتشينة] | warak liib [kotshīnæ] |
| postcards | كروت بوستال | korūt postāl |
| refill (for a pen) | أنبوبة حبر جاف | onbūbit ḥibr gāēf |
| rubber | أستيكة [ممحاة] | æstīkæ [mimḥæh] |
| rubber bands | أستيــك | æstik |
| ruler | مسطرة | mastara |
| sketching block | كراس سكتش | korrās skitch |
| stamps | طوابع بريد | tawābi' bærīd |
| string | خيط [دوبار] | khēt [dobār] |
| thumb tacks | دبابيس رسم | dæbæbīs ræsm |
| tissue paper | ورق كلينكس | warak kliniks |
| typewriter ribbon | شريط لآلة كاتبة | shirīt li'āēlæ kāētbæ |
| typing paper | ورق لآلة كاتبة | warak li'āēlæ kāētbæ |
| wrapping paper | ورق لف | warak læff |
| writing pad | بلوك ورق | blok warak |
| Where's the guide-book section? | أين قسم «الدليل السياحى»؟ | æynæ kism "æl dælīl æl siyāēhi" |
| Where do you keep the English books? | أين قسم الكتب الانجليزية ؟ | æynæ kism æl **k**otob æl 'ingilīziyyæ |

## Camping

| | | |
|---|---|---|
| I'd like a/an/some... | ... أريد | orīd |
| axe | بالطة | balta |
| bottle-opener | فتاحة زجاجات | fættāḥit zogægāt |
| bucket | جردل [سطل] | gærdæl [satl] |
| butane gas | أنبوبة بوتاجاز | onbūbit botægāz |
| camp cot | سرير للسفر | sirīr lil safar |
| camping equipment | معدات تخييم | mo'iddāt tækhyīm |
| can opener | فتاحة علب | fættāḥit 'ilæb |
| candles | شمع | shæm' |
| (folding) chair | كرسى (بلاج) | korsi (plāzh) |
| compass | برجل [بيكار] | bærgæl [bikār] |
| corkscrew | بّريمة لفتح الزجاجات | bærrimæ lifætḥ æl zogægāt |
| crockery | أطباق | atbāk |
| cutlery | فضية | faddiyyæ |
| first-aid kit | علبة اسعافات أولية | ilbitt is'āfāt æwwæliyyæ |
| flashlight | بطارية | battāriyyæ |
| frying pan | طاسة | tāsa |
| groundsheet | خيمة | khēmæ |
| hammer | شاكوش | shækūsh |
| hammock | سرير معلق | sirīr mo'allak |
| ice-bag | كيس ثلج | kis tælg |
| kerosene | كيروسين | kirosīn |
| kettle | غلاية | gællāyæ |
| lamp | لمبة | lamba |
| lantern | مصباح | misbāḥ |
| matches | كبريت [شحيطة] | kæbrit [shaḥḥēta] |
| mattress | مرتبة | mærtæbæ |
| methylated spirits | كحول | koholl |
| mosquito net | ناموسية | næmūsiyyæ |
| paraffin | كيروسين | kirosīn |
| penknife | مطوة | matwa |

| picnic case | صندوق للرحلات | sondūk lil riḥlāēt |
| primus stove | وابور جاز | wabūr gāēz |
| rope | حبل | ḥæbl |
| rucksack | شنطة للظهر | shanta lil dahr |
| saucepan | حلة | ḥællæ |
| screwdriver | مفك | mifækk |
| sheathknife | مطوة | matwa |
| sleeping bag | كيس للنوم | kis lil nōm |
| stove | فرن | forn |
| (folding) table | ترابيزة [طاولة] (للبلاج) | tarabēza [tawla] (lil plāēzh) |
| tent | خيمة | khēmæ |
| tent pegs | أوتاد خيمة | æwtāēd khēmæ |
| tent poles | عواميد خيمة | æwæmīd khēmæ |
| thermos flask (bottle) | ترموس | tirmos |
| tin opener | فتاحة علب | fættāēḥit 'ilæb |
| tongs | زرادية | zarradiyyæ |
| torch | بطارية | battāriyya |
| water carrier | حامل للماء | ḥāēmil lilmāēh' |
| wood alcohol | كحول | koḥoll |

## Crockery

| cups | فناجيل | fænægīl |
| food box | علبة طعام | ilbit taām |
| plates | أطباق | atbāk |
| saucers | أطباق للفرن | atbāk lil forn |

## Cutlery

| forks | شوك | showæk |
| knives | سكاكين | sækækīn |
| spoons | ملاعق | mælāēik |
| (made of) plastic | بلاستيك | plastik |
| (made of) stainless steel | معدنية | mæ'dæniyyæ |

## Chemist's (drugstore)

In the Middle East, chemists normally don't stock the great range of goods that you'll find in England or the U.S. In the window you'll see a notice telling you where the nearest all-night chemist's is.

For reading ease, this section has been divided into two parts:

1. Pharmaceutical—medicine, first-aid, etc.
2. Toiletry—toilet articles, cosmetics.

## General

| | | |
|---|---|---|
| Where's the nearest chemist's? | أين أقرب أجزخـانة [فرماشية] ؟ | æynæ akrab ægzækhǣnæ [færmæshiyyæ] |
| What time does the chemist open/close? | متى تفتح / تقفل الاجزخانة [الفرماشية] ؟ | mætæ tæftæḥ/takfil æl ʾægzækhǣnæ [æl færmæshiyyæ] |

## Part 1—Pharmaceutical

| | | |
|---|---|---|
| I want something for... | أريد شيئاً لـ ... | orīd shæyʾæn li |
| Can you recommend something for...? | هل يمكنك أن تنصحني بشيء لـ ... ؟ | hæl yomkinæk æn tænsaḥni bi shæyʾin li |
| a cold/a cough | برد / سعال | bærd/soǣl |
| a hangover | دوخة | dōkhæ |
| sunburn | ضربة شمس | darbit shæms |
| travel sickness | دوار السفر | dowār ælsafar |
| Can you make up this prescription? | هل يمكنك أن تجهز لى هذه الروشيتة ؟ | hæl yomkinæk æn togæhhiz li hǣzihi æl roshittæ |
| Shall I wait? | هل أنتظر ؟ | hæl antazir |
| When shall I come back? | متى أرجع ؟ | mætæ argaa |

FOR DOCTORS, see page 162

| English | Arabic | Transliteration |
|---|---|---|
| Can I get it without a prescription? | هل يباع بلا روشيتة ؟ | hæl yobāæ bilā roshittæ |
| Can I have a/an/ some...? | أريد ... | orīd |
| antiseptic cream | كريم مطهر | krēm motahhir |
| Band-Aids | شريط لاصق | shirīt lāsik |
| bandage | رباط ـ شاش | robāt-shāsh |
| chlorine tablets | حبوب كلور | hobūb klōr |
| corn plasters | شريط للكالو | shirīt lil kallo |
| cotton wool | قطن طبى | kotn tibbī |
| cough drops | نقط للسعلة | no'at lil sæælæ |
| diabetic lozenges | سكارين | sækærin |
| disinfectant | مطهر | motahhir |
| ear drops | نقط للاذن | no'at lil 'ozon |
| Elastoplast | شريط لاصق | shirīt lāsik |
| eye drops | قطرة للعيون | katra lil oyūn |
| flea powder | بودرة للبراغيث | bodra lil bærægīt |
| gargle | غرغرة | gargara |
| gauze | شاش | shāsh |
| insect lotion | لوسيون ضد الحشرات | losyōn did æl hasharāt |
| insect repellent | طارد للحشرات | tārid lil hasharāt |
| iodine | يــود | yōd |
| laxative | ملين | molæyyin |
| mouthwash | غسيل للفم | gæsīl lil fæm |
| quinine tablets | أقراص كينين | akrās kinīn |
| sanitary napkins | فوط ورق طبى | fowatt warak tibbī |
| sleeping pills | حبوب منومة | hobūb monæwwimæ |
| stomach pills | أقراص للهضم | akrās lil hadm |
| thermometer | ترمومتر | tirmomitr |
| throat lozenges | أقراص للزور | akrās lil zōr |
| tissues | غيارات | giyarāt |
| tranquillizers | أقراص مهدئة | akrās mohæddi'æ |
| vitamin pills | أقراص فيتامين | akrās vitæmīn |

## Part 2—Toiletry

| | | |
|---|---|---|
| I'd like a/an/some... | ... أريد | orīd |
| acne cream | كريم لحب الشباب | krēm liḥæbb æl shæbāeb |
| after-shave lotion | لوسيون بعد الحلاقة | losyōn baad æl ḥilāka |
| astringent | قابض | kābid |
| bath salts | أملاح للحمام | æmlāeḥ lil ḥæmmāem |
| cologne | كلونيا | kolonyāe |
| cream | كريم | krēm |
| cleansing cream | كريم للتنظيف | krēm lil tanzīf |
| cold cream | كولد كريم | kold krēm |
| cuticle cream | كريم لسطح الجلد | krēm li satḥ æl gild |
| foundation cream | كريم أساسى | krēm æsāesī |
| moisturizing cream | كريم مرطب | krēm morattib |
| night cream | كريم لليل | krēm lil lēl |
| deodorant | مزيل لرائحة العرق | mozīl li rā'iḥæt æl 'arak |
| emery board | مبرد أظافر كرتون | mabrad azāfir kartōn |
| eye pencil | قلم كحل للعين | kalam koḥl lil ēn |
| eye shadow | ظل للعيون | zill lil oyūn |
| face flannel | فوطة لتنظيف الوجه | fūta litanzīf æl wægh |
| face powder | بودرة للوجه | bodra lil wægh |
| foot cream/powder | كريم / بودرة للقدم | krēm/bodra lil kadam |
| hand cream/lotion | كريم / لوسيون لليد | krēm/losyōn lil yædd |
| Kleenex | كلينكس | kliniks |
| lipsalve | ملون للشفايف | molæwwin lil shæfāeyif |
| lipstick | روج للشفايف | rūzh lil shæfāeyif |
| make-up remover pads | قصائص مزيلة للتواليت | kasā'is mozīlæ lil twāelitt |
| mascara | كحل | kohl |
| nail brush | فرشاة للاظافر | forshæ lil azāfir |
| nail clippers | أصافة للاظافر | 'assāfa lil azāfir |
| nail file | مبرد أظافر | mabrad azāfir |
| nail polish | ملمع للاظافر | molæmmi' lil 'azāfir |
| nail polish remover | مزيل للون الاظافر | mozīl lilōn æl 'azāfir |

| | | |
|---|---|---|
| nail scissors | مقص للاظافر | makass lil azāfir |
| oil | زيت | zēt |
| perfume | عطر | itr |
| powder | بودرة | bodra |
| powder puff | بخاخة بودرة | bækhkhǣkhit bodra |
| razor blades | أمواس حلاقة | æmwǣs ḥilǣka |
| rouge | أحمر شفاة | aḥmar shifǣh |
| shampoo | شامبو | shæmpū |
| shaving brush | فرشاة للحلاقة | forshæ lil ḥilǣka |
| shaving cream | كريم للحلاقة | krēm lil ḥilǣka |
| shaving soap | صابون للحلاقة | sabūn lil ḥilǣka |
| soap | صابون | sabūn |
| sponge | سفنجة | sæfingæ |
| sun-tan cream/oil | كريم / زيت للشمس | krēm/zēt lil shæms |
| talcum powder | بودرة تلك | bodra tælk |
| toilet paper | ورق تواليت | warak twælitt |
| toilet water | ماء للتواليت | mǣʾ lil twælitt |
| toothbrush | فرشاة للاسنان | forshæ lil æsnǣn |
| toothpaste | معجون للاسنان | mæægūn lil æsnǣn |
| towel | فوطة | fūta |
| wash cloth | فوطة لتنظيف الوجه | fūta litanzīf æl wægh |

## For your hair

| | | |
|---|---|---|
| brush | فرشاة | forshæ |
| colouring | صبغة | sabga |
| comb | مشط | misht |
| curlers | لفائف للتمويج | læfǣʾif lil tæmwīg |
| grips | ماسكات [بنس] | mǣsikǣt [binæss] |
| lacquer | حافظ التسريحة ( لاكيه ) | ḥāfiz æl tæsrīḥæ (lækēh) |
| (bobby) pins | دبابيس للشعر | dæbæbīs lil shaar |
| setting lotion | سائل للتسريح | sǣʾil lil tæsrīḥ |

## Clothing

If you want to buy something specific, prepare yourself in advance. Look at the list of clothing on page 118. Get some idea of the colour, material and size you want. They're all listed in the next few pages.

## General

| | | |
|---|---|---|
| I'd like... | أريد ... | orīd |
| I want ... for a 10-year-old boy/girl. | أريد ... لولد / لبنت عمره ١٠ سنوات . | orīd...liwælæd/libint omro 10 sænæwæt |
| I want something like this. | أريد شيئاً مثل هذا . | orīd shæy'æn misl hæzæ |
| I like the one in the window. | يعجبنى ما فى الفيترينة . | yoʻgiboni mæ fil vitrīnæ |
| How much is that per metre? | بكم المتر من هذا ؟ | bikæm æl mitr min hæzæ |

| | | | |
|---|---|---|---|
| 1 centimetre | = 0.39 in. | 1 inch | = 2.54 cm. |
| 1 metre | = 39.37 in. | 1 foot | = 30.5 cm. |
| 10 metres | = 32.81 ft. | 1 yard | = 0.91 m. |

## Colour

| | | |
|---|---|---|
| I want something in... | أريد لون ... | orīd lōn |
| I want a darker/lighter shade. | أريده أغمق / أفتح . | orīd ægmak/æftæḥ |
| I want something to match this. | أريد شيئاً يناسب هذا . | orīd shæy'æn yonæsib hæzæ |
| I don't like the colour. | لا يعجبنى اللون . | læ yoʻgiboni æl lōn |

| | | |
|---|---|---|
| beige | بيج | bēzh |
| black | أسود | æswæd |
| blue | أزرق | æzrak |
| brown | بنى | bonni |
| cream | كريم | krēm |
| emerald | أخضر زمردى | akhdarr zomorrodi |
| golden | ذهبى | zæhæbi |
| green | أخضر | akhdarr |
| grey | رمادى | romādi |
| orange | برتقالى | bortokāli |
| pink | وردى | wærdi |
| purple | بنفسجى | bænæfsigi |
| red | أحمر | aḥmar |
| scarlet | أحمر غامق [نبيذى] | aḥmar gāmik [nibīti] |
| silver | فضى | faddi |
| white | أبيض | abyad |
| yellow | أصفر | asfar |

**مخطط**
(mokhattat)

**منقط**
(monakkat)

**مربعات**
(morabbaāt)

**مزركش**
(mozarkash)

## Material

| | | |
|---|---|---|
| Have you anything in...? | هل عندك قماش ... ؟ | hæl indæk komāsh |
| Is that...? | هل هذا ... ؟ | hæl hāēzæ |
| hand-embroidered | مشغول باليد | mæshgūl bil yæd |
| hand-made | شغل يد | shogl yæd |
| made here | مصنوع هنا | masnū honāē |

## What's it made of?

| | | |
|---|---|---|
| brocade | بروكار | brokār |
| cambric | تيل خفيف | til khæfif |
| camel hair | وبر الجمل | wabar gæmæl |
| chiffon | شيفون | shifōn |
| corduroy | قطيفة مضلعة | katīfa modallaa |
| cotton | قطن | kotn |
| damask | دماسيه | dæmæsē |
| felt | جوخ | gūkh |
| flannel | فانلة | fænillæ |
| gabardine | جبردين | gæbærdīn |
| lace | دانتيل | dæntillæ |
| leather | جلد | gild |
| linen | كتان [تيل] | kittāēn [til] |
| pique | قطن | kotn |
| poplin | بوبلين | poplīn |
| rayon | حرير صناعى | ḥærīr sinā'i |
| rubber | كاوتش | kæwitch |
| silk | حرير | ḥærīr |
| suede | شاموا | shæmwā |
| taffeta | تفتاه | tæftæ |
| terrycloth | قماش مسامى | omāēsh mæsāēmi |
| velvet | قطيفة | katīfa |
| wool | صوف | sūf |

## Size

| | | |
|---|---|---|
| I take size... | مقاسى ... | makāsi |
| Could you measure me? | هل يمكن أن تقيس لى ؟ | hæl yomkin æn takīs li |
| I don't know your sizes. | لا أعرف مقاساتكم . | lāē aarif makasatkom |

In that case, look at the charts on the next page.

## This is your size

### Ladies

| Dresses/Suits | | | | | | |
|---|---|---|---|---|---|---|
| US | 10 | 12 | 14 | 16 | 18 | 20 |
| Britain | 32 | 34 | 36 | 38 | 40 | 42 |
| Middle East | 42 | 44 | 46 | 48 | 50 | 52 |

| Stockings | Shoes | | | |
|---|---|---|---|---|
| US | 6 | 7 | 8 | 9 |
| Britain — sizes are the same | 4 | 5 | 6 | 7 |
| Middle East | 37 | 38 | 40 | 41 |

### Gentlemen

| Suits/Overcoats | | | | | | Shirts | | | |
|---|---|---|---|---|---|---|---|---|---|
| US / Britain | 36 | 38 | 40 | 42 | 44 | 46 | 15 | 16 | 17 | 18 |
| Middle East | 46 | 48 | 50 | 52 | 54 | 56 | 38 | 41 | 43 | 45 |

| Shoes | | | | | | | | |
|---|---|---|---|---|---|---|---|---|
| US / Britain | 5 | 6 | 7 | 8 | 8 | 9 | 9 | 10 | 11 |
| Middle East | 38 | 39 | 41 | 42 | 43 | 43 | 44 | 44 | 45 |

Sizes may vary somewhat from country to country, so the above must be taken as an approximate guide.

### A good fit?

| Can I try this on? | هل يمكن أن أقيس هذا ؟ | hæl **yom**kin æn a**kis** h**ǣ**zæ |
|---|---|---|
| Where's the fitting room? | أين حجرة القياس ؟ | æynæ ḥograt æl kiyǣs |
| Is there a mirror? | هل توجد مراية ؟ | hæl **tū**gæd mir**ǣ**yæ |

FOR NUMBERS, see page 175

| It fits very well. | . المقاس مضبوط جدا | æl makās madbūt giddæn |
| It doesn't fit. | . المقاس ليس مضبوطاً | æl makās læysæ madbūt |
| It's too... | انه ... جداً ... | innæho...giddæn |
| short/long | قصير / طويل | kasir/tawīl |
| tight/loose | ضيق / واسع | dayyik/wāēsii |
| How long will it take to alter? | متى ينتهى التصليح ؟ | mætæ yæntæhi æl taslih |

## Shoes

| I'd like a pair of... | ... أريد | orīd |
| shoes/sandals/boots | حذاء / صندل / بوط | hizā'/sandal/bōt |
| These are too... | انه ... جداً | innæho...giddæn |
| narrow/wide | ضيق / واسع | dayyik/wāēsii |
| large/small | كبير / صغير | kæbīr/sagīr |
| Do you have a larger size? | هل عندك مقاس أكبر ؟ | hæl indæk makās akbar |
| I want a smaller size. | . أريد مقاس أصغر | orīd makās asgar |
| Do you have the same in...? | ... هل عندك لون | hæl indæk lōn |
| brown/beige | بنى / بيج | bonni/bēzh |
| black/white | أسود / أبيض | æswæd/abyad |

Shoes worn out? Here's the key to getting them fixed again...

| Can you repair these shoes? | هل يمكنك اصلاح هذا الحذاء ؟ | hæl yomkinæk islāh hāēzæ æl hizāē' |
| Can you stitch this? | هل يمكنك تخييط هذا ؟ | hæl yomkinæk takhyīt hāēzæ |
| I want new soles and heels. | . أريد نعل وكعب جديدين | orīd nææl wæ kæææb gædidēn |
| When will they be ready? | متى تكون جاهزة ؟ | mætæ tækūn gæhzæ |

118

## Clothes and accessories

| I'd like a/an/some... | ... أريد | orīd |
|---|---|---|
| bath robe | برنس | bornos |
| bathing cap | بونيه للبحر | bonē lil baḥr |
| bathing suit | بدلة بحر [مايوه] | bædlit baḥr [mæyō] |
| blazer | جاكتة بليزر | zhækittæ blēzær |
| blouse | قميص حريمى | amīs ḥærīmi |
| boots | بوط | bōt |
| bow tie | كرافاته بابيون | karavatta papyōn |
| bra | حامل صدر [سوتيان] | ḥǣmil sadr [sūtyǣn] |
| braces (Br.) | حمالات | hæmmælǣt |
| briefs | لباسات [شناتين] | libæsǣt [shnætīn] |
| cap | كاسكتة | kæskittæ |
| cape | كابة [حرملة] | kǣbæ [ḥarmala] |
| coat | معطف | mi'taf |
| costume | بدلة | bædlæ |
| dinner jacket | بدلة سموكنج | bædlæ smōking |
| dress | فستان | fostǣn |
| dressing gown | روب | rōb |
| evening dress | فستان للسهرة | fostǣn lil sahra |
| fur coat | معطف فرو | mi'taf farw |
| girdle | حزام | ḥizǣm |
| gloves | جوانتى [كفوف] | gowænti [kfūf] |
| handkerchief | منديل | mændīl |
| hat | قبعة | kobbaa |
| jacket | جاكتة | zhækittæ |
| jeans | بنطلون «بلوجين» | bantalōn blū zhinz |
| jersey | بلوفر | polōvar |
| jumper (Br.) | بلوفر | polōvar |
| nightdress | قميص نوم | kamīs nōm |
| panty-girdle | كورسيه | korsē |
| panty hose | شراب حريمى طويل | shorāb ḥærīmi tawīl |

| pyjamas | بيجامة | pizhǣmæ |
| raincoat | معطف مطر | mi'taf matar |
| sandals | صندل | sandal |
| scarf | اشارب | isharp |
| shirt | قميص | kamīs |
| shoes | حذاء [سباط] | ḥizǣ' [sobbāt] |
| shorts (Br.) | شورت | short |
| skirt | جوب | jūp |
| socks | شراب [كالسات] | shorāb [kælsǣt] |
| stockings | شراب حريمى | shorāb ḥærīmi |
| suit (man's) | بدلة | bædlæ |
| suit (woman's) | فستان | fostǣn |
| suspenders | حمالة | ḥæmmǣlæ |
| sweater | جاكتة | zhækittæ |
| tennis shoes | حذاء رياضى | ḥizǣ' riyādi |
| tie | كرافات | kravāt |
| tights | شراب حريمى طويل | shorāb ḥærīmi tawīl |
| trousers | بنطلون | bantalōn |
| underpants (men) | لباسات [شناتين] | libæsǣt [shnætīn] |
| undershirt | فانلة | fænillæ |
| vest (Am.) | صديرى | sidēri |
| vest (Br.) | فانلة | fænillæ |
| waistcoat | صديرى | sidēri |

| belt | حزام | ḥizǣm |
| buckle | توكة | tōkæ |
| button | زرار | zorār |
| collar | ياقة | yǣka |
| pocket | جيب | gēb |
| shoe laces | رباط أحذية | robāt æḥziyæ |
| zip (zipper) | سوستة | sostæ |

120

## Electrical appliances and accessories—Records

There is no standard voltage within any single Middle-Eastern country, let alone throughout the region as a whole. The voltages are, in general: 110–220 volts AC, 50 cycles in Egypt (220 volts in central Cairo); 220 volts AC, 50 cycles in Jordan; and 110 volts AC, 50 cycles in Lebanon. So check before you plug your appliance in. The plug in use throughout the Middle East is the two-round-pin type.

| | | |
|---|---|---|
| What's the voltage? | كم الفولت ؟ | kæm æl volt |
| I want a plug for this. | أريد بريزة لهذا . | orīd prīzæ lihǣzæ |
| Do you have a battery for this. | هل عندك بطارية لهذا ؟ | hæl indæk battāriyyæ lihǣzæ |
| This is broken. Can you repair it? | هذا مكسور . هل يمكنك اصلاحه ؟ | hǣzæ mæksūr. hæl yomkinæk islāḥoh |
| When will it be ready? | متى يكون جاهزاً ؟ | mǣtæ yækūn gǣhizæn |
| I'd like a/an/some… | أريد … | orīd |
| adapter | بريزة أمريكانى | prīzæ æmrikǣni |
| battery | بطارية | battāriyyæ |
| blender | خلاط | khallāt |
| food mixer | خلاط | khallāt |
| hair dryer | منشف الشعر [سشوار] | monæshshif shaar [sishwār] |
| iron | مكواة | mækwæ |
| kettle | غلاية | gællǣyæ |
| plug | بريزة | prīzæ |
| radio | راديو | radyo |
| portable | ترانزيستور | tranzistor |
| record player | بيك آب | pik-ap |
| portable | ترانزيستور | tranzistor |
| shaver | ماكينة حلاقة | mækinit ḥilāka |
| speakers | مكبرات صوت | mokæbbirǣt sōt |

| | | |
|---|---|---|
| tape recorder | ريكوردر | rikordær |
| cassette | كاسيت | kasitt |
| toaster | توستر | tostær |
| transformer | محول [ترانس] | moḥæwwil [trans] |

## Record shop

| | | |
|---|---|---|
| Do you have any records by... | هل عندك اسطوانات لـ ..؟ | hæl indæk istiwanāt li |
| Can I listen to this record? | أريد أن أسمع هذه الاسطوانة من فضلك . | orīd æn æsmæ' hǣzihi æl istiwāna min fadlak |
| I'd like a cassette. | أريد كاسيت . | orīd kasitt |
| I want a new stylus. | أريد ابرة جديدة . | orīd ibra gædīdæ |

| | | |
|---|---|---|
| 33 rpm | ٣٣ لفة | tælǣtæ wæ tælætin læffæ |
| 45 rpm | ٤٥ لفة | khæmsæ wæ ærbi'in læffæ |
| mono/stereo | مونو / ستريو | mōno/stiryō |

| | | |
|---|---|---|
| Arabic music | موسيقى عربية | mūsīka arabiyyæ |
| classical music | موسيقى كلاسيك | mūsīka klǣsik |
| folk music | موسيقى فولكلورية | mūsīka folklōriyyæ |
| instrumental music | موسيقى | mūsīka |
| jazz | موسيقى جاز | mūsīka zhǣz |
| light music | موسيقى خفيفة | mūsīka khæfīfæ |
| orchestral music | موسيقى جماعية | mūsīka gæmæ'iyyæ |
| pop music | موسيقى غربية | mūsīka garbiyya |

Here are the names of a few popular recording artists known throughout the Middle East:

| | |
|---|---|
| **Om Kalsoum** | **Warda El Gazaeria** |
| **Fairouz** | **Sabah** |
| **Abdel Halim Hafez** | **Nagat El Saghira** |
| **Mohamed Abdel Wahab** | **Wadie El Safy** |
| **Farid El Atrash** | **Sabah Fakhri** |

122

## Hairdressing — At the barber's

| | | |
|---|---|---|
| I'm in a hurry. | أنا مستعجل . | ænæ mista'gil |
| I want a haircut, please. | أريد قص الشعر من فضلك . | orīd 'ass il **shaa**r min **fad**lak |
| I'd like a shave. | أريد حلق الذقن . | orīd ḥælk æl zækn |
| Don't cut it too short. | لا تقصه قصيراً جداً . | læ ta'**oss**o kasīran **gid**dæn |
| Scissors only, please. | المقص فقط من فضلك . | æl mæ'**ass** fakatt min **fad**lak |
| A razor cut, please. | قص بالموس من فضلك . | 'oss bil mūs min **fad**lak |
| Don't use the clippers. | لا تستعمل الماكينة . | læ tæstææmil æl **mæ**kinæ |
| Just a trim, please. | قص بسيط من فضلك . | 'ass basīt min **fad**lak |
| That's enough off. | يكفى هذا القص . | **yæk**fi hāēzæ æl 'ass |
| A little more off the... | قصر أكثر من ... | **kas**sar **ak**tar min |
| back | الخلف | æl khælf |
| neck | الخلف | æl khælf |
| sides | الجوانب | æl gæw**āē**nib |
| top | أعلى | ææælāē |
| I don't want any oil. | لا أريد زيت [بريانتين] . | læ orīd zēt [briyantīn] |
| Would you please trim my...? | أريد توضيب الـ ... من فضلك . | orīd taw**dib** æl...min **fad**lak |
| beard | ذقن | zækn |
| moustache | شنب | **shæ**næbb |
| sideboards (sideburns) | سوالف | sæw**āē**lif |
| Thank you. That's fine. | شكرا . هذا حسن . | **shok**ran. hāēzæ ḥæsin |
| How much do I owe you? | كم الحساب ؟ | kæm æl ḥis**āē**b |
| This is for you. | هذا لك . | hāēzæ læk |

# Ladies' hairdressing

| | | |
|---|---|---|
| Is there a hairdresser's in the hotel? | هل يوجد صالون تجميل فى الفندق ؟ | hæl **yū**gæd sal**ōn** tægm**ī**l fil **fon**dok |
| Can I make an appointment for some-time on Thursday? | أريد موعداً ليوم الخميس من فضلك . | or**ī**d **mæw**'id liy**ō**m æl **khæmī**s min **fad**lak |
| I'd like it cut and shaped. | أريد قص و تسريح . | or**ī**d 'ass wæ tæsr**ī**ḥ |
| with a fringe (bangs) | بفرانجة من الامام | bi **fran**zha minæl 'æm**ā**m |
| a razor cut | قص بالموس | 'ass bil **mū**s |
| a re-style | تسريحة جديدة | tæsr**ī**ḥæ gæd**ī**dæ |
| with ringlets | ببوكلات | bi bokl**ā**t |
| with waves | مموج | mom**æww**æg |
| in a bun | شينيون | shiny**ō**n |
| I want (a)... | أريد ... | or**ī**d |
| bleach | ازالة اللون | iz**ā**lit æl l**ō**n |
| colour rinse | غسيل باللون | gæs**ī**l bil l**ō**n |
| dye | صباغة [تلوين] | sib**ā**ga [tæl**wī**n] |
| permanent | برماننت | pirma**na**nt |
| shampoo and set | شامبو و تسريح | sham**pū** wæ tæsr**ī**ḥ |
| tint | لون | l**ō**n |
| touch up | لمسات | læmæs**ā**t |
| the same colour | نفس اللون | næfs æl l**ō**n |
| a darker colour | لون أغمق | l**ō**n **æg**mak |
| a lighter colour | لون أفتح | l**ō**n **æf**tæḥ |
| auburn/blond/ brunette | بنى / أشقر / أسود | **bon**nī/**ash**'ar/**æs**wæd |
| Do you have a colour chart? | هل عندك دليل للالوان ؟ | hæl **in**dæk dæl**ī**l lil ælw**ā**n |
| I want a... | أريد ... | or**ī**d |
| manicure/pedicure | مانيكير / بديكير | mæni**kū**r/pidi**kū**r |
| face-pack | شد للوجه | shædd lil wægh |

FOR DAYS OF THE WEEK, see page 181

## Jeweller's—Watchmaker's

Since the days of the pharaohs, handcrafting jewellery has been considered an honoured profession. Moreover, a woman's social status was reflected in the number of jewels she wore. In the markets and jewellery shops of the Middle East, you'll find excellent copies of ancient jewellery—slave bracelets, bangles, snake-shaped bracelets, bedouins' necklaces. Due to cheap local labour, you'll be pleasantly surprised at how inexpensive much jewellery can be. Don't forget, this is the occasion to try your skill at haggling.

| | | |
|---|---|---|
| Can you repair this watch? | هل يمكنك اصلاح هذه الساعة ؟ | hæl yomkinæk islāḥ hāēzihi æl sāēæ |
| The ... is broken. | ال ... مكسور . | æl...maksūr |
| glass/spring | زجاج / زمبلك [سوستة] | zogāēg/zæmbælik [sostæ] |
| strap/winder | أستيك / مسمار | ostēk/mosmār |
| I want this watch cleaned. | أريد تنظيف هذه الساعة . | orīd tanzīf hāēzihi æl sāēæ |
| When will it be ready? | متى تكون جاهزة ؟ | mætāē tækūn gæhzæ |
| Could I please see that? | من فضلك اكشف على هذا . | min fadlak ikshif ælæ hāēzæ |
| I want a small present for... | أريد هدية صغيرة لـ ... | orīd hædiyyæ sagīra li |
| I don't want anything too expensive. | لا أريد شيئاً غالياً . | læ orīd shæy'æn gāēliyæn |
| I want something... | أريد شيئاً ... | orīd shæy'æn |
| better/cheaper/ simpler | أحسن / أرخص / أبسط | æḥsæn/arkhas/absat |
| Is this real silver? | هل هذا فضة حقيقية ؟ | hæl hāēzæ fidda ḥakikiyya |
| Have you anything in gold? | هل عندك شيئاً من ذهب ؟ | hæl indæk shæy'an min zæhæb |
| How many carats is this? | كم قيراط ؟ | kæm kirāt |

When you go to a jeweller's, you've probably got some idea of what you want beforehand. Find out what the article is made of and then look up the name for the article itself in the following lists.

## What's it made of?

| | | |
|---|---|---|
| alabaster | الباستر | alabastar |
| amethyst | رجمشت | rægmæsht |
| brass | نحاس أصفر | niḥās asfar |
| copper | نحاس | niḥās |
| coral | مرجان | morgān |
| crystal | كريستال | kristāl |
| cut glass | زجاج مشكل | zogāg moshækkæl |
| diamond | الماس | almās |
| ebony | أبنوس | æbænōs |
| emerald | زمرد | zomorrod |
| enamel | صدف | sadaf |
| glass | زجاج | zogāg |
| gold | ذهب | zæhæb |
| gold plate | مذهب | mozæhhæb |
| ivory | عاج | āg |
| jade | جاد | zhād |
| mother-of-pearl | صدف | sadaf |
| onyx | عقيق | akīk |
| pearl | لولى | lūli |
| pewter | معدن | mæædæn |
| platinum | بلاتين | plātīn |
| ruby | ياقوت | yāʾūt |
| sapphire | ياقوت أزرق | yāʾūt æzrak |
| silver | فضة | fidda |
| silver plate | مفضض | mofaddad |
| topaz | زبرجد | zæbærgæd |
| turquoise | فيروز | færūz |

126

## What is it?

| English | Arabic | Transliteration |
|---|---|---|
| beads | خرز | **khar**azz |
| bracelet | غويشة | gi**wē**shæ |
| brooch | بروش | **brō**sh |
| chain | سلسلة | sil**si**læ |
| charm | حلية | **ḥil**yæ |
| cigarette case | علبة سجاير | **il**bit sæg**ǣ**yir |
| cigarette lighter | ولاعة [قداحة] | wæll**ǣ**æ [ædd**ǣ**ḥæ] |
| clock | ساعة حائط | s**ǣ**'it ḥā'it |
|   alarm clock | منبه | min**æb**bih |
| cross | صليب | sal**īb** |
| cuff-links | زراير قمصان | za**rā**yir kom**sān** |
| cutlery | فضية للاكل | fad**di**yya lil 'ækl |
| earrings | حلق | **ḥæ**læk |
| jewel box | علبة جواهر | **il**bit gæ**wǣ**hir |
| necklace | عقد | okd |
| pendant | علِّيقة | oll**ē**'æ |
| pin | دبوس | dæb**būs** |
| powder compact | علبة بودرة | **il**bit **bod**ra |
| ring | خاتم | **khǣ**tim |
|   engagement ring | دبلة خطوبة | **dib**lit kho**tū**ba |
|   puzzle ring | خاتم من قطع كثيرة | **khǣ**tim min **ki**taa kæs**ī**ra |
|   signet ring | خاتم رجالى | **khǣ**tim ri**gæ**li |
|   wedding ring | دبلة | **dib**læ |
| rosary | سبحة [مسبحة] | **sib**ḥæ [mæs**bæ**ḥæ] |
| silverware | فضية | fad**di**yya |
| strap | غويشة | gow**ē**shæ |
|   watch strap | أستيك ساعة | os**tēk** s**ǣ**æ |
| tie-clip | دبوس كرافات | dæb**būs** kra**vāt** |
| watch | ساعة | s**ǣ**æ |
|   pocket watch | ساعة جيب | s**ǣ**'it gēb |
|   wrist-watch | ساعة يد | s**ǣ**'it yædd |

## Laundry—Dry cleaning

If your hotel doesn't have its own laundry/dry cleaning service, ask the porter:

| | | |
|---|---|---|
| Where's the nearest laundry/dry cleaner's? | أين أقرب محل غسيل ومكوة / تنظيف ؟ | æynæ akrab mæḥæll gæsil wæ **mæk**wæ / tanzif |
| I want these clothes... | أريد ... هذه الملابس . | orid...hæzihi æl mælæbis |
| cleaned | تنظيف | tanzif |
| pressed/ironed | مكوة | mækwit |
| washed | غسيل | gæsil |
| When will it be ready? | متى تكون جاهزة ؟ | mætæ tækūn gæhizæ |
| I need it... | أريدها ... | oridohæ |
| today | اليوم | æl yōm |
| tomorrow | بكرة | bokra |
| before Thursday | قبل يوم الخميس | kabl yōm æl khæmis |
| Can you ... this? | أريد ... هذا من فضلك . | orid...hæzæ min fadlak |
| mend/patch/stitch | رفة / ترقيع / خياطة | ræffit/tærki'/khiyātit |
| Can you sew on this button? | هل يمكنك أن تخيط لى هذا الزر [زرار] ؟ | hæl yomkinæk æn tokhayyit li hæzæ æl zirr [zorār] |
| Can you get this stain out? | هل يمكنك ازالة هذه البقعة ؟ | hæl yomkinæk izælit hæzihi æl bokaa |
| Can this be invisibly mended? | هل يمكنك رفة هذا دون أن يظهر ؟ | hæl yomkinæk ræffit hæzæ dūnæ æn yazhar |
| This isn't mine. | هذا ليس ملكى . | hæzæ læysæ milki |
| There's one piece missing. | ناقص قطعة . | nākis kit'a |
| There's a hole in this. | يوجد ثقب [خرم] فى هذا . | yūgæd sokb [khorm] fi hæzæ |
| Is my laundry ready? | هل غسيلى جاهز ؟ | hæl gæsili gæhiz |

128

## Photography—Cameras

The basic still and home movie exposures are usually given in English in the instructions with the roll.

| | | |
|---|---|---|
| I want an inexpensive camera. | أريد كاميرا رخيصة . | orīd kæmira rakhīsa |

## Film

| | | |
|---|---|---|
| I'd like a... | ... أريد | orīd |
| cartridge | كارتردج [خزنة الفيلم] | kartridzh [khæznit ilfilm] |
| film for this camera | فيلم لهذه الكاميرا | film lihæzihi æl kæmira |
| a ... film | ... فيلم | film |
| 120 | ١٢٠ | miyyæ wæ 'ishrīn |
| 127 | ١٢٧ | miyyæ sæb'æ wæ 'ishrīn |
| 135 | ١٣٥ | miyyæ khæmsæ wæ tælætīn |
| 620 | ٦٢٠ | sottomiyyæ wæ 'ishrīn |
| 8-mm | ٨ مم | tæmænyæ milli |
| super 8 | سوبر ٨ مم | sūpar tæmænyæ milli |
| 16-mm | ١٦ مم | sittāshar milli |
| 20 exposures | ٢٠ صورة | 'ishrīn sūra |
| 36 exposures | ٣٦ صورة | sittæ wæ tælætīn sūra |
| this ASA/DIN number | درجة الحساسية ازا / دين | daragit il ḥæsāsiyyæ aza/dīn |
| fast/fine grain | سريع / قليل الحساسية | særīi/kalīl æl ḥæsāsiyyæ |
| black and white | أسود وأبيض | 'iswid wabyad |
| colour | ألوان | 'ælwǣn |
| colour negative | نجاتيف بالالوان | nigætif bil 'ælwǣn |
| colour slide | سلايد بالالوان | slayd bil 'ælwǣn |
| artificial light type | للضوء الصناعى | lil dō' æl sinā'i |
| daylight type | لضوء النهار | lidō' æl nahār |

FOR NUMBERS, see page 175

## Processing

| | | |
|---|---|---|
| How much do you charge for developing? | ؟ بكم التحميض | bikæm æl taḥmīd |
| I want ... prints of each negative. | أريد ... صورة من كل سلبية [ نجاتيف ] . | orīd...sūra min kol sælbiyyæ [nigætif] |

## Accessories

| | | |
|---|---|---|
| I want a/an/some... | ... أريد | orīd |
| cable release | مفتاح التصوير الآلى | moftæḥ æl taswīr æl'āēli |
| exposure meter | مقياس فتحة العدسة | mikyās fætḥit æl'ædæsæ |
| flash bulbs | لمبات الفلاش | lambāt æl flāēsh |
| flash cubes | لمبات فلاش مكعبة | lambāt flāēsh mokæ'æbæ |
| filter | فلتر | filtar |
| red/yellow | أحمر / أصفر | 'aḥmar/'asfar |
| ultra violet | فوق البنفسجى | fō' æl bænæfsigi |
| lens cap | غطاء العدسة | gitā' æl'ædæsæ |
| lens cleaners | منظف للعدسة | monazzif lil'ædæsæ |

## Broken

| | | |
|---|---|---|
| Can you repair this camera? | هل يمكنك اصلاح هذه الكاميرا ؟ | hæl yomkinæk 'islāḥ hēzihi æl kæmira |
| The film is jammed. | الفيلم محشور . | æl film maḥshūr |
| There's something wrong with the... | ال ... عطلان . | æl...'atlān |
| exposure counter | عداد الصور | 'æddāēd æl sowar |
| film winder | مفتاح لف الفيلم | moftæḥ læff æl film |
| lens | عدسة | 'ædæsæ |
| light meter | مقياس الضوء | mikyāēs æl dō' |
| rangefinder | ضابط المسافة | dābit æl mæsāēfæ |
| shutter | منظم فتحة العدسة | monazzim fætḥit æl 'ædæsæ |

130

## Provisions

| I'd like a/an/some... please. | . أريد ... من فضلك | orīd...min fadlak |
|---|---|---|
| apples | تفاح | toffǣḥ |
| bananas | موز | mōz |
| beer | بيرة | bīræ |
| biscuits (Br.) | بسكويت | bæskæwit |
| bread | عيش [خبز] | ēsh [khobz] |
| butter | زبدة | zibdæ |
| cake | كيك | kēk |
| candy | حلويات | ḥælæwiyyǣt |
| cheese | جبنة | gibnæ |
| chocolate | شيكولاته | shokolāta |
| coffee | قهوة [بن] | kahwa [bonn] |
| cold cuts | لحوم باردة | loḥūm bærdæ |
| cookies | بسكويت | bæskæwit |
| cooking fat | سمن | sæmnæ |
| cream | كريمة | krēmæ |
| eggs | بيض | bēd |
| ice-cream | آيس كريم [جيلاتي] | æys krēm [zhilāti] |
| lemonade | لمونادة | læmonǣtæ |
| lemons | ليمون [حامض] | læmūn [ḥāmid] |
| lettuce | خس | khass |
| milk | لبن حليب | læbæn ḥælīb |
| mustard | مستردة | mostarda |
| oranges | برتقال | bortokāl |
| pepper | فلفل [بهار] | filfil [bohār] |
| potatoes | بطاطس | batātis |
| rolls | خبز سندوتش | khobz sændæwitsh |
| salad | صلاطة | salāta |
| salt | ملح | mælḥ |
| sandwiches | سندوتش | sændæwitsh |
| sausages | سوسيس [سجق/معانق] | sōsis [sogo'/mæ'ǣnik] |

| | | |
|---|---|---|
| sugar | سكر | sokkar |
| sweets | حلويات | hælæwiyyǣt |
| tea | شاى | shǣy |
| tomatoes | طماطم [بندورة] | tamātim [banadūra] |
| yogurt | زبادى [لبن] | zæbǣdi [læbæn] |

# And don't forget...

| | | |
|---|---|---|
| a bottle opener | فتاحة زجاجات | fættǣḥit zogǣgǣt |
| a corkscrew | فتاحة علب | fættǣḥit ilæb |
| matches | كبريت [شعيطة] | kæbrīt [shaḥḥātæ] |
| paper napkins | فوط. ورق | fowatt wæræk |
| a tin (can) opener | فتاحة علب | fættǣḥit ilæb |

| Weights and measures |
|---|
| 1 kilogram or kilo (kg) = 1000 grams (g) |
| 100 g = 3.5 oz.  ½ kg = 1.1 lb.  1 oz. =  28.35 g |
| 200 g = 7.0 oz.  1 kg = 2.2 lb.  1 lb. = 453.60 g |
| |
| 1 litre (l) = 0.88 imp. quarts = 1.06 U.S. quarts |
| 1 imp. quart  = 1.14 l    1 U.S. quart  = 0.95 l |
| 1 imp. gallon = 4.55 l    1 U.S. gallon = 3.8  l |

| | | |
|---|---|---|
| box | علبة | ilbæ |
| carton | صندوق كارتون | sondūk kartōn |
| jar | أبريق | æbrī' |
| packet | باكو | bǣko |
| tin (can) | علبة صفيح | ilbæ safīḥ |
| tube | أنبوبة | onbūbæ |
| gram | جرام | grām |
| pound | رطل | ratl |
| kilogram | كيلوجرام | kilogrām |
| litre | لتر | litr |

## Souvenirs

Browsing through the bustling markets will turn up count-
less treasured souvenirs of your visit to the Middle East.
Jewellery and precious stones will certainly interest the
ladies. Ceramics, glassware, sandals and hand-embroidered
garments also make especially appreciated gifts.

Below are a few suggestions for souvenirs you might like to
bring home:

| | | |
|---|---|---|
| antiques | انتيكات | æntik**ǣ**t |
| backgammon set | طاولة زهر | ta**w**lit zahr |
| brass and copper objects | مصنوعات نحاس | masnū´āt niḥǣs |
| carpets | سجاجيد | sægǣg**i**d |
| ceramics | فخار | fokh**kh**ār |
| cutlery (Lebanon) | فضية | fad**d**iyya |
| dagger | خنجر | **kh**angar |
| glass (hand-blown) | زجاج | zogǣg |
| gold filigree | ذهب مشغول | dæhæb mæsh**g**ūl |
| hand-embroidered garments | ملابس تطريز يدوى | mælǣbis ta**tr**iz y**æ**dæwi |
| handicrafts | صناعات يدوية | sinaāt gil**d**iyyæ |
| jewellery | مجوهرات | mogawharāt |
| kaftan | قفطان | koft**ā**n |
| leather goods | مصنوعات جلدية | masnū´āt gil**d**iyyæ |
| nargile (water pipe) | شيشة [أرجيلة] | sh**ī**shæ [ærg**ī**læ] |
| oriental lamp | مصباح شرقى | misbāḥ **sh**arki |
| sandals | صندل | **s**andal |
| silver jewel box | علبة جواهر فضة | **i**lbit gæwǣhir fad**d**a |
| stones, precious | أحجار كريمة | aḥgār kær**ī**mæ |
| semi-precious | شبه كريمة | shibh kær**ī**mæ |
| tarboosh (fez) | طربوش | tarb**ū**sh |
| Turkish coffee service | طقم للقهوة التركى | takm lil **kah**wa æl **tor**ki |

## Tobacconist's

You'll find the typical oriental cigarettes (e.g., *Cleopatra* in Egypt, *Bafra* or *Khanon* in Lebanon) lighter than those at home. The reason is that the young tobacco leaves are harvested before they mature. Brands that are manufactured locally are quite cheap. Foreign cigarettes are considerably more expensive.

| | | |
|---|---|---|
| Give me a/an some..., please. | أريد ... من فضلك . | orīd... min **fadl**ak |
| cigars | سيجار | sig**ā**r |
| cigarette case | علبة لحمل السجاير | 'ilbæ liḥæml æl sægā̈yir |
| cigarette holder | فم سجاير | fomm sægā̈yir |
| flints | حجر ولاعة [قداحة] | ḥagar wællā̈æ ['ædd**ā̈**ḥæ] |
| lighter | ولاعة [قداحة] | wællā̈æ ['ædd**ā̈**ḥæ] |
| lighter fluid/gas | بنزين/غاز ولاعة [قداحة] | bænz**ī**n /g**ā**z wællā̈æ ['ædd**ā̈**ḥæ] |
| matches | كبريت [شحيطة] | kæb**rī**t [shaḥḥ**ē**ta] |
| packet of cigarettes | علبة سجاير | 'ilbit sægā̈yir |
| packet of *Cleopatras* | علبة كليوباترة | 'ilbit kily**ō**batra |
| pipe | بايب | payp |
| pipe tobacco | دخان بايب | dokhkaā̈n payp |
| pipe cleaners | منظف بايب | mo**nazz**if payp |
| tobacco pouch | باكو دخان بايب | b**ā̈**ko dokhkh**ā̈**n payp |
| Have you any...? | عندك ... ؟ | **æn**dæk |
| American cigarettes | سجاير أمريكانى | sægā̈yir 'æmrik**ā̈**nī |
| English cigarettes | سجاير انجليزى | sægā̈yir 'ingil**ī**zi |
| menthol cigarettes | سجاير منتول | sægā̈yir min**to**l |
| I'd like a carton. | أريد خرطوشة . | orīd khart**ū**sha |

| | | |
|---|---|---|
| filter-tipped | بفم فلتر | bi**fo**mm **fil**tær |
| without filter | بدون فلتر | bid**ū**n **fil**tær |

# Your money: banks—currency

In the Middle East, there's generally no import limit on foreign currency. In Egypt, on the other hand, no Egyptian currency may be brought in or taken out of the country, and all foreign currency brought in must be declared. When you change money, don't forget to ask for a receipt or have the transaction noted on your D (declaration) form. When leaving Egypt, customs will ask you either for your receipts or your D form.

## Monetary unit

**Egypt:**  1 Egyptian pound (£E) = 100 piastres (pts.) = 1,000 mil.

**Jordan:**  1 Jordanian dinar (JD) = 1,000 fils (fls.)

**Lebanon:** 1 Lebanese pound (£L) = 100 piastres (pts.)

| | Bank-notes | Coins |
|---|---|---|
| **Egypt** | 5, 10, 25, 50 pts. 1, 5, 10£E | ½, 1, 5, 10 pts. |
| **Jordan** | 500 fls.; 1, 5, 10, 50 JD | 1, 5, 10, 20, 50, 100 fls. |
| **Lebanon** | 1, 5, 10, 25, 50, 100 L£ | 1, 2½, 5, 10, 25, 50 pts. |

## Banking hours

**Egypt:**  8.30 a.m. − 12.30 p.m., daily except Friday; Sunday 10 a.m. to noon.

**Jordan:**  8.30 a.m. − 1 p.m. and 3.30 p.m. − 7.30 p.m.; Saturday to Thursday.

**Lebanon:** 8.30 a.m. − 12.30 p.m., Monday to Friday; Saturday 8.30 a.m. − 12 a.m.

## Before going

| | | |
|---|---|---|
| Where's the nearest...? bank/currency exchange? | أين أقرب بنك / مكتب كامبيو ؟ | æynæ 'akrab bænk / mæktæb kæmbyo |
| Where can I cash a traveller's cheque (check)? | أين يمكن صرف شيكات سياحية ؟ | æynæ yomkin sarf shēkāt siyāḥiyyæ |
| Where's the American Express? | أين الأميريكان اكسبريس؟ | æynæ æl 'æmirikæn iksprēs |

## Inside

| | | |
|---|---|---|
| I want to change some dollars/pounds. | أريد تحويل دولارات / جنيهات استرلينى . | orīd tæḥwīl dolārāt / gonæyhāt 'istirlīni |
| What's the exchange rate? | ما سعر التحويل ؟ | mæ siir æl tæḥwīl |
| What rate of commission do you charge? | ما العمولة التى يأخذها البنك ؟ | mæ æl 'omulæ ællæti yæ'khozohæ æl bænk |
| Can you cash a personal cheque? | هل تصرف شيكات خاصة ؟ | hæl tasrif shēkāt khāssa |
| How long will it take to clear? | ما طول مدة المراجعة ؟ | mæ tūl moddit æl moræg'æ |
| Can you wire my bank in London? | هل يمكنك أن ترسل تلغراف الى بنكى فى لندن ؟ | hæl yomkinæk æn torsil tælligrāf 'ilæ bænki fi landan |
| I have... | عندى ... | 'indi |
| a letter of credit | خطاب ضمان | khitāb damān |
| an introduction from... | خطاب من ... | khitāb min |
| a credit card | بطاقة رصيد مصرفى | bitākit rasīd masrafi |
| I'm expecting some money from... Has it arrived yet? | أنا منتظر فلوس من ... هل وصلت ؟ | ænæ montazir folūs min... hæl wasalæt |
| Please give me... 10-pound notes (bills) and some small change. | من فضلك اعطنى ... ورقة من فئة العشرة جنيهات وبعض الفكَّـة [الفراطة] | min fadlak aatini... waraka min fi'æt 10 gonæyhāt wa baad æl fækkæ [æl frāta] |

| Give me...large notes and the rest in small notes. | اعطنى ... ورقة من فئة كبيرة والباقى فئآت صغيرة. | aatini... waraka min fi´æ kæbiræ wæl bāki fi´āt sagira |
| Could you please check that again? | من فضلك راجع هذا . | min fadlak rāgii hāæzæ |
| I want to credit this to my account. | أريد ايداع هذا فى حسابى . | orid ´idāæ hāæzæ fi hisāæbi |
| Where should I sign? | أين أوقع ؟ | æynæ owakki´ |

## Currency converter

In a world of fluctuating currencies, we can offer no more than this do-it-yourself chart. You can get a card showing current exchange rates from banks, travel agents and tourist offices. Why not fill in this chart, too, for handy reference?

| | £ | $ |
|---|---|---|
| 10 Egyptian piastres<br>50<br>1 Egyptian pound<br>5<br>10 | | |
| 100    Jordanian fils<br>500<br>1 Jordanian dinar<br>5<br>10 | | |
| 1 Lebanese pound<br>5<br>10<br>50<br>100 | | |

## At the post office

In Egypt post offices are open from 8.30 a.m. to 3 p.m. except Sundays when they open only in the morning. They remain closed all day Friday. Big hotels usually have all post office facilities at the reception.

In Jordan the post offices are open from 8 a.m. to 2 p.m. except Friday when they are closed all day.

In Lebanon, mail, telex and telegram service is available from 8.30 a.m. to 1 p.m. except Friday. At least in Beirut, you can telephone from the post office 24 hours a day.

| | | |
|---|---|---|
| Where's the nearest post office? | أين أقرب مكتب بريد ؟ | æynæ akrab mæktæb bærid |
| What time does the post office open/ close? | متى يفتح / يقفل مكتب البريد ؟ | mætæ yæftæḥ/yakfil mæktæb æl bærid |
| What window do I go to for stamps? | أين شباك الطوابع ؟ | æynæ shibbǣk æl tawābii |
| At which counter can I cash an international money order? | فى أى شباك يمكننى صرف حوالة بريدية أجنبية ؟ | min æyy shibbǣk yomkinoni sarf howǣlæ bæridiyyæ ægnæbiyyæ |
| I want some stamps, please. | أريد طوابع من فضلك . | orīd tawābi' min fadlak |
| What's the postage for a letter to England? | بكم الخطاب لانجلترا ؟ | bikǣm ælkhitāb li 'ingiltira |
| What's the postage for a postcard to the U.S.A.? | ما الثمن لارسال كارت بوستال الى أمريكا ؟ | mǣ æltæmæn li 'irsǣl kǣrt postǣl 'ilæ 'æmrīkæ |

| | |
|---|---|
| طوابع | STAMPS |
| طرود | PARCELS |
| حوالات بريدية | MONEY ORDERS |

| | | |
|---|---|---|
| Do all letters go airmail? | هل كـل الخطابات تسافر بالبريد الجوى ؟ | hæl koll æl khitābāt tosææfir bil bærīd æl gæwwi |
| I want to send this parcel. | أريد ارسال هذا الطرد . | orīd 'irsāl hææzæl tard |
| Do I need to fill in a customs declaration? | هل يجب أن أملأ استمارة الجمرك ؟ | hæl yægib æn 'æmlæ' 'istimārit æl gomrok |
| Where's the mailbox? | أين صندوق الخطابات ؟ | æynæ sondūk æl khitābāt |
| I want to send this by... | أريد ارسال هذا ... | orīd 'irsāl hææzæ |
| airmail | بالبريد الجوى | bil bærīd æl gæwwī |
| express (special delivery) | بالبريد المستعجل | bil bærīd æl mostææægæl |
| registered mail | بالبريد المسجل | bil bærīd æl mosæggæl |
| Where's the poste restante (general delivery)? | أين مكتب تسليم الخطابات ؟ | æynæ mæktæb tæslim æl khitābāt |
| Is there any mail for me? My name is... | هل توجد خطابات لى ؟ اسمى ... | hæl tūgæd kitābāt li? 'ismi |
| Here's my passport. | هذا باسبورى . | hææzæ paspōri |

## Telegrams

| | | |
|---|---|---|
| I want to send a telegram. May I please have a form? | أريد ارسال تلغراف . من فضلك اعطنى استمارة . | orīd 'irsāl tælligrāf. min fadlak aatini 'istimāra |
| How much is it per word? | بكم الكلمة ؟ | bikæm æl kilmæ |
| How long will a cable to Boston take? | متى يصل التلغراف الى بوسطون ؟ | mætæ yasil æl tælligrāf 'ilæ boston |
| I'd like to reverse the charges. | أريد أن يدفع المستلم ثمن التلغراف . | orīd 'æn yædfææ æl mostælim tæmæn æl tælligrāf |
| I'd like to send a letter-telegram (night-letter). | أريد ارسال تلغراف L. T. . | orīd 'irsæl tælligrāf æl ti |

## Telephoning

You won't find any telephone booths in Egypt and Jordan except at the post office. When you want to make a local call, you can go into a store. If you want to call long distance, you'll have to go to a post office or a big hotel.

In Lebanon calls can be made from telephone booths or from restaurants, cafés or hotels. Public telephones are coin operated: insert the appropriate coins and then dial. When the other person answers, push the white button to complete the connection.

| | | |
|---|---|---|
| Where's the telephone? | أين التليفون ؟ | æynæl tilifōn |
| May I use your phone? | هل يمكنني استعمال التليفون ؟ | hæl yomkinoni 'istiimāel æl tilifōn |
| Do you have a telephone directory of Beirut? | هل عندك دليل تليفونات بيروت ؟ | hæl 'indæk dælil tilifōnāet bæyrūt |
| Can you help me get this number? | من فضلك ساعدني فى الاتصال بهذا الرقم . | min fadlak sāe'idni fil 'ittisāl bihāēzæ æl rakam |

## Operator

| | | |
|---|---|---|
| Do you speak English? | هل تتكلم انجليزى ؟ | hæl tætækællæm ingilīzi |
| Good morning, I want Cairo 123 456. | صباح الخير . أريد القاهرة ١٢٣٤٥٦ . | sabāḥ æl khēr. orīd ælkāhira 123 456 |
| Can I dial direct? | هل يوجد خط مباشر ؟ | hæl yūgæd khatt mobāēshir |
| I want to place a personal (person-to-person) call. | أريد مكالمة شخصية . | orīd mokælmæ shakhsiyyæ |
| I want to reverse the charges. | أريد أن يدفع الشخص المطلوب ثمن المكالمة . | orīd æn yædfææ æl shakhs æl matlūb tæmæn æl mokælmæ |
| Will you tell me the cost of the call afterwards? | هل يمكنك أن تخبرنى بثمن المكالمة فيما بعد ؟ | hæl yomkinæk æn tokhbirni bitæmæn æl mokælmæ fimæ bææd |

## Speaking

| | | |
|---|---|---|
| Hello. This is... speaking. | آلو . أنا .. | ælō. ʾænæ |
| I want to speak to... | أريد أن أتحدث الى ... | orīd æn ʾætæḥæddæs ʾilæ |
| Would you put me through to...? | من فضلك اعطنى ... ؟ | min **fad**lak aatini |
| I want extension... | أريد الداخلى رقم ... | orīd æl dækhili rakam |
| Is that...? | هل هذا ... ؟ | ˙hæl **hæ**zæ |

## Bad luck

| | | |
|---|---|---|
| Would you please try again later? | من فضلك حاول مرة أخرى فيما بعد . | min **fad**lak ḥæwil **mar**ra ʾokhra fimæ **bæ**æd |
| Operator, you gave me the wrong number. | لقد أعطيتنى نمرة غلط . | **la**kad aataytæni **nim**ræ galat |
| Operator, we were cut off. | انقطعت المكالمة . | ʾinkataʾæt æl mo**kæl**mæ |

## Not there

| | | |
|---|---|---|
| When will he/she be back? | متى يرجع / ترجع ؟ | mætæ **yær**gaa/**tær**gaa |
| Will you tell him/her I called? | من فضلك قل له / لها انى اتصلت . | min **fad**lak kol læho/læhæ inni itta**salt** |
| My name's... | اسمى ... | **is**mi |
| Would you ask him/her to call me? | من فضلك اطلب منه / منها الاتصال بى . | min **fad**lak otlob **min**ho/ **min**hæ æl ʾitti**sāl** bi |
| Would you please take a message? | من فضلك خذ هذه الرسالة . | min **fad**lak khozz **hæ**zihi æl ri**sæ**læ |

## Charges

| | | |
|---|---|---|
| What was the cost of that call? | بكم هذه المكالمة ؟ | bik**æ**m h**ā̈**zihi **æ**l mok**æ**lmæ |
| I want to pay for the call. | أريد أن أدفع ثمن المكالمة . | orid 'æn 'æ**d**fææ t**æ**mæn æl mok**æ**lmæ |

---

| | |
|---|---|
| توجد مكالمة تليفونية لك . | There's a telephone call for you. |
| ما النمرة التى تطلبها ؟ | What number are you calling? |
| الخط مشغول . | The line's engaged. |
| لا يرد أحد . | There's no answer. |
| النمرة غلط . | You've got the wrong number. |
| التليفون عطلان . | The phone is out of order. |
| هو خرج / هى خرجت . | He's/She's out at the moment. |

FOR SPELLING, see page 11

# The car

## Filling station

We'll start this section by considering your possible needs at
a filling station.

| | | |
|---|---|---|
| Where's the nearest filling station? | أين أقرب محطة بنزين ؟ | æynæ akrab maḥattit bænzīn |
| I want...litres of petrol (gas), please. | أريد ... لتر بنزين من فضلك . | orīd...litr bænzīn min fadlak |
| ten/twenty/fifty | عشرة / عشرين / خمسين | 'ashara/'ishrīn/khæmsīn |
| I want...litres of standard/premium. | أريد ... لتر بنزين عادى / سوبر . | orīd...litr bænzīn 'ædi/ sūpar |
| Fill the tank, please. | املأها من فضلك . | imlæhæ min fadlak |
| Please check the oil and water. | من فضلك اكشف على الزيت والماء . | min fadlak ikshif ælæ æl zēt wæl mæ' |
| Give me...litres of oil. | اعطنى ... لتر زيت . | 'ātīni...litr zēt |
| Fill up the battery with distilled water. | املأ البطارية بماء مقطَّر . | imlæ' æl battāriyya bimayya mokattara |
| Check the brake fluid. | اكشف على زيت الفرامل . | ikshif ælæ zēt æl farāmil |

| Fluid measures | | | | | |
|---|---|---|---|---|---|
| litres | imp. gal. | U.S. gal. | litres | imp. gal. | U.S. gal. |
| 5 | 1.1 | 1.3 | 30 | 6.6 | 7.9 |
| 10 | 2.2 | 2.6 | 35 | 7.7 | 9.2 |
| 15 | 3.3 | 4.0 | 40 | 8.8 | 10.6 |
| 20 | 4.4 | 5.3 | 45 | 9.9 | 11.9 |
| 25 | 5.5 | 6.6 | 50 | 11.0 | 13.2 |

**FOR NUMBERS, see page 175**

| | | |
|---|---|---|
| Would you check the tires? | من فضلك اكشف على ضغط العجل [الدواليب] . | min **fadl**ak '**ik**shif 'æl**ǣ** dagt æl '**æ**gæl [æl dwæ**lib**] |
| The pressure should be 23 front, 26 rear. | الضغط. ٢٣ للأمام و ٢٦ للخلف | æl dagt 23 lil 'æm**ǣ**m wæ 26 lil khælf |
| Check the spare tire, too, please. | من فضلك اكشف على الاستبن . | min **fadl**ak '**ik**shif 'æl**ǣ**l '**is**tibn |
| Can you mend this puncture (fix this flat)? | من فضلك اصلح هذه العجلة [الدولاب] . | min **fadl**ak '**asl**ih h**ǣ**zihi æl '**æ**gælæ [æl d**ūlǣ**b] |
| Will you change this tire, please? | من فضلك غيّر هذه العجلة [الدولاب] . | min **fadl**ak g**æ**yyir h**ǣ**zihi æl '**æ**gælæ [æl d**ūlǣ**b] |
| Will you clean the windshield (windscreen)? | من فضلك نظف الزجاج الأمامى . | min **fadl**ak **nazz**if æl zog**ǣ**g æl '**æ**m**ǣ**mi |
| Have you a road map of this area? | هل عندك خريطة للطرق فى هذه المنطقة . | hæl '**ind**æk kharita lil **tor**ok fi h**ǣ**zihi æl mantika |
| Where are the toilets? | أين التواليت ؟ | **æyn**æl tw**æ**lit |

## Asking the way—Street directions

| | | |
|---|---|---|
| Excuse me. | من فضلك ! | min **fadl**ak |
| Can you tell me the way to...? | ما هو الطريق الى ... ؟ | m**ǣ** howæ æl tar**ik** '**ilǣ** |
| How do I get to...? | كيف أصل الى ... ؟ | k**ǣ**yfæ '**asil** '**ilǣ** |
| Where does this road lead to? | الى أين يؤدى هذا الطريق ؟ | '**ilæ** '**æyn**æ yo'**æ**ddi h**ǣ**zæ æl tar**ik** |
| Can you show me on this map where I am? | من فضلك اشير لى على مكانى على الخريطة . | min **fadl**ak '**æ**shir li 'æl**ǣ** mæk**ǣ**ni 'æl**æ**l kharita |
| How far is it to... from here? | ما هى المسافة الى ... | m**ǣ** hiyæ æl mæs**ǣ**fæ '**ilǣ** |

| Miles into kilometres | | | | | | | | | |
|---|---|---|---|---|---|---|---|---|---|
| 1 mile = 1.609 kilometres (km) | | | | | | | | | |
| miles | 10 | 20 | 30 | 40 | 50 | 60 | 70 | 80 | 90 | 100 |
| km | 16 | 32 | 48 | 64 | 80 | 97 | 113 | 129 | 145 | 161 |

| Kilometres into miles | | | | | | | | | | | | |
|---|---|---|---|---|---|---|---|---|---|---|---|---|
| 1 kilometre (km) = 0.62 miles | | | | | | | | | | | | |
| km | 10 | 20 | 30 | 40 | 50 | 60 | 70 | 80 | 90 | 100 | 110 | 120 | 130 |
| miles | 6 | 12 | 19 | 25 | 31 | 37 | 44 | 50 | 56 | 62 | 68 | 75 | 81 |

| انك على طريق غلط . | You're on the wrong road. |
|---|---|
| أذهب الى الأمام . | Go straight ahead. |
| انه هناك على الشمال ( اليمين ) . | It's down there on the left (right). |
| اذهب من هذا الطريق ... | Go that way. |
| اذهب الى أول ( ثانى ) تقاطع . | Go to the first (second) crossroads. |
| انعن الى الشمال ( اليمين ) عند الاشارة . | Turn left (right) at the traffic lights. |

In the rest of this section we'll be more closely concerned with the car itself. We've divided it into two parts:

*Part A* contains general advice on motoring in the Middle East. It's essentially for reference and is therefore to be browsed over, preferably in advance.

*Part B* is concerned with the practical details of accidents and breakdown. It includes a list of car parts and a list of things that may go wrong with them. Just show it to the garage mechanic and have him point to the items required.

## Part A

### Customs—Documentation

Visitors will require the following documents to get their car through customs:

Passport and visa
International driving licence
Car registration papers (log book)*
Tryptic (customs pass booklet for vehicle); not required in Lebanon if you are travelling on a tourist visa

Insurance requirements vary from country to country:

*Egypt* requires that tourists obtain insurance in order to drive in the country. The International Motor Insurance Certificate (Green Card) is recognized only if Egypt is specifically mentioned on the document. If you haven't taken out an insurance extension before leaving home, you can get coverage at your arrival point in Egypt or through the Egyptian Touring Club Association.

*Lebanon* has no compulsory insurance requirements, but the Green Card is recognized provided Lebanon is specifically mentioned on the document. Insurance can also be obtained upon arrival through an insurance company in Beirut.

*Jordan* has no compulsory insurance requirements. It would be advisable, before leaving home, to have your regular insurance policy extended to cover travel in the Middle East. However, coverage can also be obtained locally if needed be.

Though the above information is up to date as we go to press, it is advisable to check with your automobile association or the appropriate consulate before you leave home.

* Egypt requires an international car registration document, obtainable through your local automobile association.

| | | |
|---|---|---|
| Here's my... | ... هذا / هذه | hǣzæ/hǣzihi |
| driving licence | رخصة القيادة | rokhsit ælkiyǣdæ |
| insurance policy | بوليصة التأمين | bolīsit æltæ'mīn |
| green card | بوليصة التأمين الدولية | bolīsit æltæ'mīn ældæwliyyæ |
| passport | باسبورى | paspōri |
| I haven't anything to declare. | ليس عندى أى شىء أعلن عنه . | læysæ 'indi 'æyy shē' 'oolin 'ænho |
| I've... | ... عندى | 'indi |
| a carton of cigarettes | خرطوشة سجاير | khartūshit sægǣyir |
| a bottle of whisky | زجاجة وسكى | zogǣgit wiskī |
| a bottle of wine | زجاجة نبيت | zogǣgit nibīt |
| We're staying for... | ... سنبقى | sænabkā |
| a week | أسبوع | 'osbū' |
| 2 weeks* | أسبوعين | 'osbūēn |
| a month | شهر | shahr |

## Roads

Roads—especially main highways—in the Arab countries are generally good and road signs are usually given in English. We recommend prudent driving until you're familiar with the roads, signs and the driving habits of the local drivers. You'll find that drivers make extensive use of their horns. Don't let this scare you; just be sure to follow the traffic rules.

Pedestrian crossings are marked by white zebra stripes, but the security they seem to offer is often illusory.

Distances are marked in kilometres, and the main highways have road signs. There are rest areas *(isteraha)* at frequent intervals where you can refuel, check your car or make minor repairs while having a drink or snack.

* see grammar

Arab highways are not fenced, and night driving at high speed is dangerous, particularly on desert roads between Alexandria and Cairo where you may unconsciously stray into the desert unless you are alert to the road verge markings.

Speed limits in Arabic countries are as follows:

|  | Residential areas | Open highways |
|---|---|---|
| cars | 50 km/h (30 mph) | 90 km/h (56 mph) |
| motorcycles | 40 km/h (25 mph) | 70 km/h (44 mph) |

## Parking

Use your common sense when parking. The police are normally reasonably lenient with tourists, but don't push your luck too far. You can be fined on the spot for traffic offenses.

In Egypt, in addition to parking meters, you'll find car parks, where a versatile attendant will park your car for you, if necessary by moving other cars to create a space. He may ask you to leave your handbrake off to facilitate his work of shuffling cars around. You'll recognize him by his special badge. It's customary to give the attendant a small tip for his services.

| Excuse me. May I park here? | ممكن أركن [أصف] هنا من فضلك ؟ | momkin 'ærkin ['asiff] honǣ min fadlak |
| How long may I park here? | ما مدة الركن [الصف] المسموحة ؟ | mǣ moddit æl rækn [æl saff] æl mæsmūḥæ |
| What's the charge for parking here? | بكم الركن [الصف] هنا ؟ | bikæm æl rækn [æl saff] honǣ |
| Must I leave my lights on? | هل يجب أن أترك النور ؟ | hæl yægib 'æn 'ætrok æl nūr |

## Road signs

You'll find that many of the standard international road signs are used in the Arab countries. Some special ones are shown on pages 160–161.

Here are some of the main written signs you're likely to encounter when driving in the Middle East.

| | |
|---|---|
| الطريق يضيق | Road narrows |
| احترس | Caution |
| احترس ، أطفال | Attention, children |
| الزم اليمين | Keep right |
| تحويلة | Diversion (Detour) |
| خطر | Danger |
| طريق منزلق | Slippery road |
| طريق سريع | Motorway (Expressway) |
| عبور مشاة | Pedestrians |
| مزلقان | Level-crossing (Railroad crossing) |
| قف | Stop |
| ممنوع الانتظار | No parking |
| ممنوع الدخول | No entry |
| مستشفى | Hospital |
| منحنى خطر | Dangerous bend (curve) |
| ممنوع تغطى السيارة التى أمامك | No overtaking (No passing) |
| موقف سيارات | Parking |
| مدرسة | School |
| منطقة عمل | Road works (Men working) |
| هدوء | Silence |
| شارع اتجاه واحد | One-way street |
| هدىء السرعة | Slow |
| هدىء السرعة | Drive slowly |

FOR ROAD SIGNS, see also pages 160–161

## Part B

## Accidents

This section is confined to immediate aid. The legal problems of responsibility and settlement can be taken care of at a later stage. Your first concern will be for the injured.

| Is anyone hurt? | هل أصيب أحد ؟ | hæl osībæ 'æḥæd |
| Don't move. | لا تتحرك . | lǣ tætæḥarrak |
| It's all right. Don't worry. | لا تقلق . كل شىء على ما يرام . | læ tæ'læ'. kol shē' 'ælǣ mǣ yorām |
| Where's the nearest telephone? | أين أقرب تليفون ؟ | æynæ 'akrab tilifōn |
| Can I use your telephone? There's been an accident. | هل يمكنني استعمـال تليفونك ؟ فيه حادثه . | hæl yomkinoni 'istiimǣl tilifōnæk? fih ḥædsæ |
| Call a doctor/ ambulance quickly. | اطلب دكتور / سيارة اسعاف بسرعة . | otlob doktōr/sæyyārit 'isæǣf bisoraa |
| There are people injured. | هناك مصابون . | honǣk mosābūn |
| Help me get them out of the car. | ساعدنى على اخراجهم من السيارة . | sæ'idni 'ælǣ 'ikhrāgihim min æl sæyyāra |

## Police—Exchange of information

| Please call the police. | من فضلك اطلب البوليس . | min fadlak 'otlob æl bolīs |
| There's been an accident. It's about 3 kilometres from... | لقد وقع حادث على بعد ٣ كيلومتر من ... | lakad wakaa ḥǣdis 'ælæ bood 3 kilomitr min |
| I'm on the Cairo–Alexandria road, 25 kilometres from Alexandria. | أنا على طريق مصر – اسكندرية على بعد ٢٥ كيلومتر من الاسكندرية . | 'ænǣ ælǣ tarik masr– 'iskindiriyyæ 'ælǣ bood 25 kilomitr minæl 'iskændæriyyæ |
| Here's my name and address. | هذا اسمى وعنوانى . | hǣzæ 'ismī wæ 'innǣni |

| Would you mind acting as a witness? | هل يمكنك أن تشهد ؟ | hæl yomkinæk 'æn tæshhæd |
| I'd like an interpreter. | أريد مترجم . | orīd motærgim |

Remember to put out a red triangle warning if the car is out of action or impeding traffic.

## Breakdown

...and that's what we'll do with this section: break it down into four phases.

1. *On the road*
   You ask where the nearest garage is.

2. *At the garage*
   You tell the mechanic what's wrong.

3. *Finding the trouble*
   He tells you what he thinks is wrong.

4. *Getting it fixed*
   You tell him to fix it and, once that's done, settle the account (or argue about it).

## Phase 1—On the road

| Where's the nearest garage? | أين أقرب جراج ؟ | æynæ 'akrab garāzh |
| Excuse me. My car has broken down. May I use your phone? | سيارتى تعطلت . هل يمكننى استخدام تليفونك من فضلك ؟ | sæyyārati ta'attalat. hæl yomkinoni 'istikhdāem tilifōnæk min fadlak |
| What's the telephone number of the nearest garage? | ما نمرة تليفون أقرب جراج ؟ | mæ nimrit tilifōn akrab garāzh |
| I've had a breakdown at... | تعطلت سيارتى عند ... | ta'attalat sæyyārati 'indæ |

| We are on the Beirut–Tripoli road, about 10 kilometres from Beirut. | نحن على طريق بيروت – طرابلس ، على بعد ١٠ كم من بيروت . | næḥno ælǣ tarik bæyrūt–tarablos ælǣ bood ashara kilomitr min bæyrūt |
|---|---|---|
| Can you send a mechanic? | من فضلك ارسل لنـا ميكانيكى . | min fadlak arsil lænǣ mikæn īki |
| Can you send a truck to tow my car? | من فضلك ارسل لنا لورى لسحب السيارة . | min fadlak arsil lænǣ lōri lisæḥb ælsayyāra |
| How long will you be? | متى ترجع ؟ | mætǣ targaa |

## Phase 2—At the garage

| Can you help me? | هل يمكنك مساعدتى ؟ | hæl yomkinæk mosǣ'æ-dæti |
|---|---|---|
| I don't know what's wrong with it. | لا أعرف ما بها . | lǣ aaraf mǣ bihǣ |
| I think there's something wrong with the... | أظن أن ... به عيب . | azonn ænnæ...bihi ēb |
| axle | محور العجلة | miḥwar æl 'ægælæ |
| battery | البطارية | æl battariyya |
| brakes | الفرامل | æl farāmil |
| clutch | الدبرياج | æl dibriyǣzh |
| contact | الكونتاكت | æl kontækt |
| dip (dimmer) switch | مفتاح النور | moftǣḥ æl nūr |
| direction indicator | الاشارة | æl 'ishāra |
| door | البـاب | æl bǣb |
| dynamo | الدينامو | æl dinamō |
| electrical system | الكهرباء | æl kahraba |
| engine | الموتور | æl motōr |
| fuel feed | خرطوم البنزين | khartūm æl bænzīn |
| gears | التروس | æl torūs |
| generator | الدينامو | æl dinæmō |
| horn | آلة التنبيه [الكلاكسون] | ǣlæt æl tænbih [klækson] |
| ignition system | المـارش | æl marsh |

| | | |
|---|---|---|
| lights | النور | æl ʿadwāʾ |
| brake lights | نور الفرامل | nūr æl farāmil |
| headlights | النور الأمامى | æl nūr æl ʿæmāēmi |
| rear (tail) lights | النور الخلفى | æl nūr æl khælfi |
| reversing (backup) lights | نور السير للخلف | nūr æl marsh khælfi |
| muffler | ماسورة العادم [الشكمان] | masūrit æl ādim [æl shækmāēn] |
| oil system | الزيت | æl zēt |
| radiator | الرادياتير | æl radiatēr |
| seat | الكرسى | æl korsi |
| silencer | ماسورة العادم [الشكمان] | masūrit æl ādim [æl shækmāēn] |
| speedometer | عداد السرعة | æddāēd æl soraa |
| starter motor | الاستارتر [المارش] | æl ʿistartir [æl marsh] |
| steering | عجلة القيادة [الدركسيون] | æ gælit æl kiyādæ [æl diriksyōn] |
| suspension | السوست [السسبنسيون] | æl sosæt [æl sospænsyōn] |
| transmission | عمود الكردان | æmūd ælkirdāēn |
| turn signal | الاشارة | æl ʿishāra |
| wheels | العجل [الدواليب] | æl ægæl [æl dwalīb] |
| wipers | المساحات | æl mæssæḥāēt |

| LEFT | RIGHT |
|---|---|
| يسار | يمين |
| (yæsār) | (yæmīn) |

| FRONT | BACK |
|---|---|
| أمــام | خلف |
| (ʿæmāēm) | (khælf) |

| | | |
|---|---|---|
| It's (too) ... | انه ... | innæho |
| backfiring | يصفق | yosaffik |
| bad | سيىء | sæyyiʾ |
| blown | ضارب | dārib |
| broken | مكسور | maksūr |
| burnt | محترق | moḥtarik |
| chafing | يحتك | yæḥtækk |
| cracked | مشقوق | mæshkūk |

| | | |
|---|---|---|
| defective | ظايــب | bāyiz |
| disconnected | غير واصل | gēr wāsil |
| dry | جــاف | gæff |
| jammed | مزنوق | mæznū′ |
| jerking | يخبط | yokhabbitt |
| knocking | يدق | yædok |
| leaking | يخر | yækhorr |
| loose | مفكوك | mæfkūk |
| noisy | يسبب صوتاً | yosæbbib sawtan |
| overheating | يسبب سخونة شديدة | yosæbbib sokhūnæ shædīdæ |
| slack | غير مشدود | gēr mæshdūd |
| slipping | ينزلق [يزحط] | yænzalik [yozaḥḥit] |
| split | منقسم | monkasim |
| stuck | مزنوق | mæznū′ |
| vibrating | يهتز | yæhtæzz |
| weak | ضعيف | da′īf |
| The car won't start. | السيارة لا تدور . | æl sayyāra læ tadūr |
| The car won't pull. | السيارة لا تسحب . | æl sayyāra læ tæsḥæb |
| The car is making a funny noise. | السيارة يها صوت غريب . | æl sayyāra bihæ sōt gærīb |
| It's locked and the keys are inside. | السيارة مقفولة والمفتاح بداخلها . | æl sayyāra mæskūkæ wæl moftāḥ bidækhilhæ |
| The radiator is leaking. | الرادياتير يخر . | æl radyatēr yækhorr |
| The clutch engages too quickly. | الدبرياج يفلت بسرعة . | æl dibriyāēzh yæflit bisoraa |
| The steering wheel's vibrating. | عجلة القيادة تهتز . | ′ægælit æl kiyāda tæhtæzz |
| The suspension is weak. | السوست [السبنسيون] ضعيفة . | æl sosætt [æl sospænsyōn] da′īfa |
| The ... needs adjusting. | ال ... محتاج الى ضبط . | æl... moḥtāg ilæ dabt |
| brake/clutch/idling | فرامل/دبرياج/سيلانسيه | farāmil/dibriyāēzh/ silansyēh |

Now that you've explained what's wrong, you'll want to know how long it will take to repair it and arrange yourself accordingly.

| How long will it take to repair? | ما مدة التصليح ؟ | mæ tūl **mod**dæt æl taslị̄ḥ |
| Suppose I come back tomorrow? | هل أرجع بكرة ؟ | hæl **ar**gaa **bo**kra |
| Can you give me a lift into town? | هل يمكنك توصيلى الى المدينة ؟ | hæl yomkinæk tawṣīli ilæ ælmædīnæ |
| Is there a place to stay nearby? | هل يوجد مكان قريب للبقاء فيه ؟ | hæl **yū**gæd mæ**kææn** karib lil ba**kā**' fih |

## Phase 3—Finding the trouble

It's up to the mechanic either to find the trouble or to repair it. All you have to do is hand him the book and point to the text in Arabic below.

من فضلك راجع القائمة التالية وأشر الى ما به عيب . واذا أراد الزبون معرفة العيب بالضبط. فابحث عن اللفظ المناسب فى القائمة التى تليها ( مكسور ، به ماس كهربائى ، الخ ... )*

| فلتر الهواء | air filter |
| البطارية | battery |
| البيلاّت | bearing |
| علبة السلندرات | block |
| قفـل | bolt |
| الفرامل | brake |
| اسطوانة الفرامل [الطمبور] | brake drum |
| تيل الفرامل [الكوليه] | brake lining |
| جهاز هيدروليكية الفرامل | brake hydraulic system |

* Please look at the following alphabetical list and point to the defective item. If your customer wants to know exactly what's wrong with it, pick the applicable term from the next list (broken, short-circuited, etc.).

| | |
|---|---|
| الفرش | brushes |
| الكابل | cable |
| عمود الكامة | crankshaft |
| الكاربراتير | carburettor |
| قميص السلندر | casing |
| الهواء | choke |
| الشاسيه | chassis |
| الدبرياج | clutch |
| اسطوانة الدبرياج | clutch plate |
| البوبينة | coil |
| الكوندنسر | condenser |
| عمود اتصال البستم | connecting (piston) rod |
| التوصيلة | connection |
| الكونتاكت | contact |
| جهاز التبريد | cooling system |
| البيلاّت | crankshaft |
| الكورونة والترس | crown wheel and pinion |
| السلندر | cylinder |
| وجه السلندرات | cylinder head |
| جوان السلندرات | cylinder head gasket |
| الغشاء | diaphragm |
| الدفرنسيال | differential |
| الدستربيوتر | distributor |
| أسلاك الدستربيوتر | distributor leads |
| الدينامو | dynamo (generator) |
| كهرباء السيارة | electrical system |
| الموتور | engine |
| سير المروحة | fan belt |
| الفلتر | filter |
| العوامة | float |
| عجلة القيادة [الدركسيون] | flywheel |
| عداد/طلمبة/خرطوم/خزان البنزين | fuel gauge/pump/feed/tank |
| العداد | gauge |

| | |
|---:|:---|
| علبة التروس | gear box |
| الاشعال | ignition coil |
| جوان | joint (packing) |
| الأسلاك | leads |
| العمود الرئيسى | main bearing |
| ماسورة العادم [الشكمان] | manifold |
| الخليط [الكاربراتير] | mixture |
| قواعد الموتور | mountings |
| تبريد/فلتر/طلمبة الزيت | oil cooler/filter/pump |
| البستم | piston |
| أماكن الاتصال | points |
| الطلمبة | pump |
| الرادياتير | radiator |
| الرباط | relay |
| السجمان — حول البستم | rings |
| شاكوش الدستربيوتر | rotor arm |
| عمود | shaft |
| الأمر تسير | shock-absorber |
| ماسك الفرامل | shoes |
| ماسورة العادم | silencer (muffler) |
| البوجيهات | sparking plugs |
| السوستة [الرفَّاص] | spring |
| بوبينة المارش | starter armature |
| المارش | starter motor |
| عجلة القيادة | steering |
| علبة عجلة القيادة | steering box |
| السوست [الرفَّاصات] | suspension |
| القلاَّب | tappet |
| الأسنان | teeth |
| الترموستات | thermostat |
| توقيت الكهرباء | timing |
| زوايا العجل | tracking |
| عمود الكردان | transmission |

| | |
|---|---|
| جوان الكردان | universal joint |
| البلف [السوباب] | valve |
| طلمبة الماء | water pump |
| العجل [الدواليب] | wheels |
| الأسلاك | wiring |

بالقــائمة التــالية بها كلمــات تدل على العيب الموجود فى السيــارة أو ما يلزم عملــه . *

| | |
|---|---|
| ضبط | to adjust |
| ضبط الاتزان | to balance |
| تفريغ | to bleed |
| مفرقع | blown |
| مكسور | broken |
| محترق | burnt |
| تغيير | to change |
| شحن | to charge |
| تنظيف | to clean |
| به صدأ – متآكل | corroded |
| مشقوق | cracked |
| عطلان | defective |
| وسخ | dirty |
| غير واصل | disconnected |
| جــاف | dry |
| خرط الصبابات | to grind in |
| عــالى | high |
| مزنوق | jammed |
| يغر | leaking |
| مفكوك | loose |
| فــك | to loosen |
| منخفض | low |
| يقطّع [الموتور] | misfiring |

* The following list contains words about what's wrong or what may need to be done with the car.

| | |
|---:|:---|
| لا يشحن | not charging |
| يسخن بشدة | overheating |
| متآكل | pitted |
| لعب | play |
| سريع | quick |
| تغيير التيلة | to reline |
| استبدال – تغيير | to replace |
| الخليط غني في الكابراتير | rich |
| به ماس كهربائي | short-circuited |
| غير مشدود | slack |
| ينزلق [يزحط] | slipping |
| فك الموتور | to strip down |
| احكام الربط | to tighten |
| ضعيف | weak |
| متآكل | worn |

# Phase 4—Getting it repaired

| | | |
|:---|---:|:---|
| Have you found the trouble? | هل وجدت العيب ؟ | hæl wægædt æl ēb |
| Is that serious? | هل هو أمر خطير ؟ | hæl howæ amron khatir |
| Can you repair it? | هل يمكنك اصلاحها ؟ | hæl yomkinæk islāḥæhā |
| Can you do it now? | هل يمكنك اصلاحها الآن ؟ | hæl yomkinæk islāḥæhā æl ʿāen |
| What's it going to cost? | كم ستتكلف ؟ | kæm sætætækællæf |

# What if he says "no"?

| | | |
|:---|---:|:---|
| Why can't you do it? | لماذا لا يمكنك اصلاحها ؟ | limāēzæ lā yomkinæk islāḥæha |
| Is it essential to have that part? | هل هذه القطعة ضرورية ؟ | hæl hāezihi æl kitaa darūriyya |

| How long is it going to take to get the spare parts? | متى يمكن الحصول على قطع الغيار ؟ | mætǣ yomkin æl hosūl ælǣ kitaa æl giyār |
| Where's the nearest garage that can repair it? | أين أقرب جراج يمكنه اصلاحها ؟ | æynæ akrab garāzh yomkinoho islāhæhæ |
| Can you fix it so that I can get as far as...? | هل يمكنك اصلاحها حتى أصل الى ... | hæl yomkinæk islāhæhæ hættǣ asill ilǣ |

If you're really stuck, ask:

| Can I leave my car here for a day/a few days? | هل أستطيع أن أترك سيارتي هنا لمدة يوم / بضعة أيام ؟ | hæl astatī æn atrok sayyarati honǣ limoddæt yōm/bidaat æyyǣm |

## Settling the bill

| Is everything fixed? | هل تم اصلاح كل شيء ؟ | hæl tæmmæ islah koll shē´ |
| How much do I owe you? | كم الحساب ؟ | kæm æl hisǣb |
| Will you take a traveller's cheque? | هل تقبل الشيكات السياحية ؟ | hæl takbæl æl shikǣt æl siyǣhiyyæ |
| Thanks very much for your help. | شكراً جزيلا على مساعدتك. | shokran gæzīlæn ælǣ mosǣˊædatikæ |
| This is for you. | هذا لك . | hǣzæ læk |

But you may feel that the workmanship is sloppy or that you're paying for work not done. Get the bill itemized. If necessary, get it translated before you pay.

| I'd like to check the bill first. Will you itemize the work done? | أريد مراجعة الحساب . من فضلك اكتب تفصيل الشغل . | orīd moragˊit æl hisǣb. min fadlak iktib tafsil æl shogl |

If the garage still won't back down–and you're sure you're right—get the help of a third party.

## Some Arabic road signs

ممنوع
الدوران للخلف

No U turn

ممنوع
الاتجاه الى الشمال

No left turn

ممنوع الدخول

No entry

ممنوع الاتجاه
الى اليمين

No right turn

أقصى حمولة

Maximum
load 10 tons

أقصى سرعة

Maximum
speed 60 kph.

أقصى ارتفاع

Maximum
height 4 m.

أقصى عرض

Maximum
width 2 m.

ممنوع
الوقوف

No stopping

طريق مغلق

Road closed

مكان الانتظار

Parking

ممنوع
الانتظار

No parking

مستشفى

Hospital

ممنوع استعمال
آلة التنبيه

No honking

ممنوع مرور
العربات

Animal-drawn
vehicles prohibited

ممنوع مرور
عربات اليد

Handcarts
prohibited

اتجاه اجبارى
One way

محطة بنزين
Petrol

ورشة تصليح
Garage

مركز اسعاف ونجدة
First-aid post

مزلقان مفتوح
Level (railroad) crossing
without barrier

أقصى عرض
Maximum
width 3 m.

أقصى ارتفاع
Maximum
height 4 m.

كوبرى متحرك
Opening or
swing bridge

مطب
Dip

طريق غير مستو
Uneven road

طريق متعرّج
Winding road

منحدر خطر
Steep hill

أمامك علامة قف
Stop at major
road ahead

تقاطع الطريق
Side road

علامة
سانت أندروز
(مزلقان سكك حديد)
Location of level
(railroad) crossing without
gate or barrier

# Doctor

Frankly, how much use is a phrase book going to be to you in the case of serious injury or illness? The only phrase you need in such an emergency is...

| Get a doctor—quick! | اطلب دكتور — بسرعة ! | otlob doktōr—bisoraa |
|---|---|---|

But there are minor aches and pains, ailments and irritations that can upset the best planned trip. Here we can help you—and, perhaps, the doctor.

Many doctors will speak English well; others will know enough for your needs. But suppose there's something the doctor can't explain because of language difficulties? We've thought of that. As you'll see, this section has been arranged to enable you and the doctor to communicate. From page 165 to 171, you'll find your side of the dialogue on the upper half of each page; the doctor's is on the lower half.

The whole section has been divided into three parts: illness, wounds, nervous tension. Page 171 is concerned with prescriptions and fees.

## General

| Can you get me a doctor? | اطلب لى دكتور من فضلك. | otlob li doktōr min fadlak |
|---|---|---|
| Is there a doctor here? | هل يوجد دكتور هنا ؟ | hæl yūgæd doktōr honæ |
| Where's there a doctor who speaks English? | أين يوجد دكتور يتكلم انجليزى ؟ | æynæ yūgæd doktōr yætækællæm ingilīzi |
| Where's the surgery (doctor's office)? | أين مكتب الدكتور ؟ | æynæ mæktæb æl doktōr |
| What are the surgery (office) hours? | ما هى مواعد العيادة ؟ | mæ hiyæ mæwæid æl 'iyāēdæ |

| Could the doctor come to see me here? | هل يستطيع الدكتور الكشف عليّ هنا ؟ | hæl yastatī æl doktōr æl kæshf allayya honā |
| What time can the doctor come? | متى يستطيع الدكتور الحضور ؟ | mætæ yastatī æl doktōr æl ḥodūr |

## Symptoms

Use this section to tell the doctor what's wrong. Basically, what he'll need to know is:

| **What?** | (ache, pain, bruise, etc.) |
| **Where?** | (arm, stomach, etc.) |
| **How long?** | (have you had the trouble) |

Before you visit the doctor find out the answers to these questions by glancing through the pages that follow.

## Parts of the body

| ankle | قصبة الرجل | kasabit æl rigl |
| appendix | المصران الأعور | æl mosrān æl 'aawar |
| arm | ذراع | zirāa |
| artery | شريان | shoryāēn |
| back | ظهر | zahr |
| bladder | مثانة | mæsāēnæ |
| blood | دم | dæmm |
| bone | عظم | azm |
| breast | ثدى | sædy |
| chest | صدر | sadr |
| collar-bone | الترقوة | æl torkowæ |
| ear | أذن | 'ozon |
| elbow | كوع | kū' |
| eye | عين | ēn |
| finger | أصبع | asbaa |

| | | |
|---|---|---|
| foot | قدم | **ka**dam |
| gland | غدة | **god**dæ |
| hand | يـــد | yædd |
| head | رأس | ra's |
| heart | قلب | kalb |
| heel | كعب | **kæ**æb |
| hip | ردف | rædf |
| intestines | مصارين | masa**rīn** |
| joint | مفصل | **mif**sal |
| kidney | كليـــة | **kil**yæ |
| knee/knee cap | ركبة / صابونة الركبة | **rok**bæ/sa**būn**it æl **rok**bæ |
| leg | ساق | **sāk** |
| liver | كبـــد | **kæ**bid |
| lung | رئــة | ri'æ |
| mouth | فم | fæm |
| muscle | عضل | 'adal |
| neck | رقبة | **ra**kabæ |
| nerve | عصب | 'asab |
| nervous system | الجهاز العصبى | æl gi**hāz** æl'asabi |
| nose | أنف | ænf |
| rib | ضلع | dil' |
| shoulder | كتف | kitf |
| skin | الجلد | æl gild |
| spine | العمود الفقرى | æl 'æ**mūd** æl **fak**ri |
| stomach | المعدة | æl mi'idæ |
| tendon | العرقوب | æl 'or**kūb** |
| throat | الزور [الزلاعيم] | æl zōr [æl zælæ**'im**] |
| toe | أصبع القدم | **as**baa æl **ka**dam |
| tongue | لسان | li**sān** |
| tonsils | اللـــوز | æl li**wæzz** |
| urine | بول | bōl |
| vein | عرق | 'irk |
| wrist | معصم | **mi**'sam |

# PATIENT
## Part 1—Illness

| English | Arabic | Transliteration |
|---|---|---|
| I'm not feeling well. | لا أشعر أنى كويس . | lǣ ash'or ænni kwæyyis |
| I've got a pain here. | عندى ألم هنا . | indi 'ælæm honǣ |
| His/Her...hurts. | عنده / عندها ألم فى ال ... | indo/indæhǣ 'ælæm fil |
| I've got (a)... | عندى ... | indī |
| headache/backache | صداع / ألم فى الظهر | sodāa/'ælæm fil dahr |
| fever/sore throat | حرارة / ألم فى الحلق | harāra/'ælæm fil holok |
| I'm constipated. | عندى امساك . | indi imsǣk |
| I've been vomiting. | عندى قىء . | indi kē' |
| I feel... | أشعر ... | ash'or |
| faint/dizzy | بضعف / بدوخة | bidaaf/bidōkhæ |
| nauseated/shivery | بصداع / برعشة | bisodāa/biraasha |

---

# DOCTOR

الجزء الأول – المرض

| Arabic | English |
|---|---|
| ما العلة ؟ | What's the trouble? |
| أين الالم ؟ | Where does it hurt? |
| منذ متى و أنت تشعر بهذا الالم ؟ | How long have you had this pain? |
| منذ متى و أنت تشعر بهذا؟ | How long have you been feeling like this? |
| شمر قميصك من فضلك . | Roll up your sleeve. |
| اخلع ملابسك (حتى الوسط ) . | Please undress (down to the waist). |
| من فضلك اخلع البنطلون و اللباس . | Please remove your trousers and underpants. |

## PATIENT

| | | |
|---|---|---|
| I've/He's/She's got (a/an)... | ...عندها / عنده / عندى | indi/indo/indæhǣ |
| abscess | دمل | dimmil |
| asthma | ربو | rabw |
| boil | خراج | khorrāg |
| chill | برد | bærd |
| cold | زكام | zokǣm |
| constipation | امساك | imsǣk |
| convulsions | تشنجات | tæshænnogǣt |
| cramps | شد عضلى | takallosāt |
| diarrhoea | اسهال | ishǣl |
| fever | حرارة | harāra |
| haemorrhoids | بواسير | bæwǣsïr |
| hay fever | زكام ربيعى | zokǣm rabïi |
| hernia | فتق | fætk |

---

## DOCTOR

| | |
|---|---|
| ارقد هنا من فضلك . | Please lie down over here. |
| افتح فمك . | Open your mouth. |
| تنفس بعمق . | Breathe deeply. |
| اسعل من فضلك . | Cough, please. |
| هل هى أول مرة تشعر بهذا ؟ | Is this the first time you've had this? |
| سأقيس درجة حرارتك . | I'll take your temperature. |
| سأقيص ضغط دمك . | I'm going to take your blood pressure. |
| سأعطيك حقنة . | I'll give you an injection. |
| أريد عينة من البول / البراز . | I want a sample of your urine/ stools. |
| سأصف لك مضاد حيوى . | I'll prescribe an antibiotic. |

## PATIENT

| | | |
|---|---|---|
| indigestion | عصر هضم | 'osr hadm |
| inflammation of... | التهاب فى ... | 'iltihāēb fi |
| influenza | انفلونزا | 'ænfilwænzæ |
| morning sickness | صداع الصباح | sodāa æl sabāh |
| rheumatism | روماتزم | romætizm |
| stiff neck | التواء فى العنق | 'iltiwāē' fil 'onok |
| sunburn | حرق من الشمس | hark min æl shæms |
| sunstroke | ضربة شمس | darbit shæms |
| tonsillitis | التهاب فى الزور [الزلاعيم] | 'iltihāēb fil zōr |
| ulcer | قرحة | korha |
| whooping cough | سعال ديكى | soæl dīki |
| It's nothing serious, I hope? | أرجو أن لا يوجد ما يدعو الى القلق . | 'argū 'ællæ yūgæd mæ yæd'ū 'ilæl kalak |

## DOCTOR

| | |
|---|---|
| لا يوجد ما يدعو الى القلق . | It's nothing to worry about. |
| عندك ... | You've got (a/an)... |
| حساسية / التهاب فى الزور [الزلاعيم] | allergy / angina |
| التهاب فى الزائدة الدودية / التهاب فى القصبة الهوائية | appendicitis / bronchitis |
| التهاب فى المثانة / دسنتريا | cystitis / dysentery |
| تسمم / الصفراء | food poisoning / jaundice |
| لمباجو / التهاب رئوى | lumbago / pneumonia |
| التهاب فى ... | an inflammation of... |
| يجب أن تذهب الى طبيب متخصص . | I want you to see a specialist. |
| يجب أن تذهب الى المستشفى لاجراء كشف عام . | I want you to go to the hospital for a general check-up. |

## PATIENT

| English | Arabic | Transliteration |
|---|---|---|
| I'm a diabetic. | عندى مرض السكر . | indi marad æl sokkar |
| I've a cardiac condition. | أنا مريض بالقلب . | ænæ marid bil kalb |
| I had a heart attack in... | أصابتنى ذبحة صدرية فى ... | asābætni zæbḥæ sadriyya fi |
| I'm allergic to... | عندى حساسية ضد ... | indi ḥæsæsiyyæ didd |
| I'd like you to prescribe some medicine for me. | اكتب لى دواء من فضلك. | oktob li dæwæ' min fadlak |
| This is my usual medicine. | هذا هو دوائى المعتاد . | hæzæ howe dæwæ'i ælmo'tæd |
| I need this medicine. | أنا محتاج لهذا الدواء . | ænæ mohtæg li hæzæ æl dæwæ |
| I'm expecting a baby. | أنا حامل . | ænæ ḥæmil |
| Can I travel? | هل يمكننى السفر ؟ | hæl yomkinoni æl safar |

---

## DOCTOR

| Arabic | English |
|---|---|
| ما كمية الانسولين التى تأخذها ؟ | What dose of insulin are you taking? |
| بحقنة أم بالفم ؟ | Injection or oral? |
| ما العلاج الذى تتبعه ؟ | What treatment have you been having? |
| ما الدواء التى تأخذه ؟ | What medicine have you been taking? |
| عندك ذبحة صدرية (خفيفة) . | You've had a (slight) heart attack. |
| لا نستعمل ... هذا مشابه له جداً . | We don't use... This is very similar. |
| متى تتوقعين الولادة ؟ | When's the baby due? |
| يجب ألا تسافرى حتى... | You can't travel until... |

## PATIENT

### Part 2—Wounds

| Could you have a look at this...? | من فضلك اكشف على هذا / هذه ... | min **fadlak ikshif** æelæ **hæ**zæ/**hæ**zihi |
|---|---|---|
| boil | الخراج | æl **khorrāg** |
| bruise | الكدمة | æl **kæd**mæ |
| burn | الحرق | æl **ḥark** |
| cut | القطع | æl kat′ |
| graze | خدش | æl **khædsh** |
| insect bite | قرصة حشرة | ′arsit **ḥashara** |
| rash | الطفح | æl **tafḥ** |
| swelling | الورم | æl **waram** |
| wound | الجرح | æl **gærḥ** |
| I can't move my... | لا أستطيع أن أحرك ... | læ astatī æn oḥærrik... |
| It hurts. | انه يؤلمنى . | innæho yo′limoni |

---

## DOCTOR

الجزء الثانى – الجروح

| انه (ليس) متلوثاً . | It's (not) infected. |
|---|---|
| عندك انزلاق غضروفى . | You've got a slipped disc. |
| يجب أن تعمل أشعة . | I want you to have an X-ray. |
| انه ... | It's... |
| مكسور / ملتوى | broken/sprained |
| متحرك من مكانه / متمزق | dislocated/torn |
| سأصف لك مطهر . | I'll give you an antiseptic. |
| ليس ما يدعو الى القلق . | It's not serious. |
| أريد أن تأتى لاراك بعد ... يوم . | I want you to come and see me in... days' time. |

## PATIENT

### Part 3—Nervous tension

| | | |
|---|---|---|
| I'm in a nervous state. | أنا فى حالة عصبية . | ænæ fi ḥælæ asabiyya |
| I'm feeling depressed. | أشعر باكتئاب . | ash'or bi'ikti'æb |
| I want some sleeping pills. | أريد حبوباً منومة . | orīd ḥobūbæn monæwwimæ |
| I can't eat. | لا أستطيع أن آكل . | læ astatī æn ækol |
| I can't sleep. | لا أستطيع أن أنام . | læ astatī æn ænæm |
| I'm having night-mares. | عندى كوابيس . | indi kæwæbīs |
| Can you prescribe a...? | هن فضلك اكتب لى... | min fadlak iktibli |
| sedative/tranquillizer | مسكن / مهدىء | mosækkin/mohæddi' |
| anti-depressant | مضاد للاكتئاب | modād lil'ikti'æb |

## DOCTOR

الجزء الثالث – التوتر العصبى

| | |
|---|---|
| عندك اجهاد عصبى . | You're suffering from nervous tension. |
| انت محتاج الى راحة . | You need a rest. |
| ما الاقراص التى تتناولها ؟ | What pills have you been taking? |
| كم قرص فى اليوم ؟ | How many a day? |
| منذ متى و أنت تشعر بهذا ؟ | How long have you been feeling like this? |
| سأصف لك بعض الاقراص | I'll prescribe some pills. |
| سأصف لك مسكناً . | I'll give you a sedative. |

## PATIENT

### Prescriptions and dosage

| | | |
|---|---|---|
| What kind of medicine is this? | ما نوع هذا الدواء ؟ | mææ nōo hǣzæ ældæwǣ' |
| How many times a day should I take it? | كم مرة فى اليوم يجب أن أتناوله ؟ | kæm **marra** fil yōm **yæ**gib æn ætænǣ**w**ælho |
| Must I swallow them whole? | هل أبتلعها كاملة ؟ | hæl æbtæli'hǣ kǣmilæ |

### Fee

| | | |
|---|---|---|
| How much do I owe you? | كم يجب أن أدفع لك ؟ | kæm **yæ**gib æn **æd**fææ læk |
| Do I pay you now or will you send me your bill? | هل أدفع لك الآن أم سترسل لى الحساب ؟ | hæl **æd**fææ læk æl'**ǣn** æm sæ**tor**sil li æl**h**i**sǣb** |
| Thanks for your help, doctor. | شكراً على مساعدتك يادكتور . | **shok**ran ælǣ mosǣ'ædætikæ yǣ dok**tōr** |

---

## DOCTOR

الجزء الرابع – العلاج والجرعة

| | |
|---|---|
| خذ ... ملعقة شاى من هذا الدواء كل ... ساعة . | Take...teaspoon(s) of this medicine every ... hours. |
| خذ ... قرص مع كوب ماء ... | Take...tablets with a glass of water... |
| *L'árabe est manquant* | ...times a day |
| قبل الطعام / بعد الطعام | before each meal/after each meal |
| فى الصباح / فى المساء | in the mornings/at night |

الحساب

| | |
|---|---|
| الحساب ... من فضلك . | That's...please. |
| من فضلك ادفع الآن . | Please pay me now. |
| سأرسل لك الحساب . | I'll send you a bill. |

## Dentist

| | | |
|---|---|---|
| Can you recommend a good dentist? | من فضلك انصحنى بطبيب أسنان جيد . | min **fadl**ak insaḥni bitab**ī**b æsn**ǣ**n gæyyid |
| Can I make an (urgent) appointment to see Dr....? | أريد موعداً (عاجلاً) مع الدكتور ... | or**ī**d maw'id**æ**n ('**ǣ**gil**æ**n) maal dokt**ō**r |
| Can't you possibly make it earlier than that? | ألا يمكن أن يكون الموعد قبل ذلك ؟ | 'æl**ǣ yom**kin æn yæk**ū**n æl **maw**'id kabl z**ǣ**lik |
| I've a toothache. | عندى ألم فى أسنانى . | indi 'æl**æ**m fi æsn**ǣ**ni |
| I've an abscess. | عندى خراج . | indi khorr**ā**g |
| This tooth hurts. | هذه السنة تؤلمنى . | h**ǣ**zihi æl **sin**næ to'li**mo**ni |
| at the top | الى أعلى [ فوق ] | il**ǣ** 'æ**æl**ǣ [f**ō**k] |
| at the bottom | الى أسفل [ تحت ] | il**ǣ æs**fæl [tæḥt] |
| in the front | الى الامام | il**ǣ** æl '**æmǣ**m |
| at the back | الى الخلف | il**ǣ** æl kh**æ**lf |
| Can you fix it temporarily? | هل يمكنك علاجها مؤقتاً ؟ | hæl **yom**kinæk il**ǣ**gæh**ǣ** mo'ak**ka**tæn |
| I don't want it extracted. | لا أريد خلعها . | l**ǣ** or**ī**d kh**æ**l'ih**ǣ** |
| I've lost a filling. | سقط حشو السنة . | sakata ḥ**æ**shw æl **sin**næ |
| The gum is... | اللثة ... | æl **l**æsæ |
| very sore | تؤلمنى بشدة | to' li**mo**ni bi**shid**dæ |
| bleeding | تنزف | t**æn**zif |

## Dentures

| | | |
|---|---|---|
| I've broken this denture. | كسرت هذا الطقم . | kas**a**rt h**ǣ**zæ æl **takm** |
| Can you repair this denture? | هل يمكنك اصلاح هذا الطقم ؟ | hæl **yom**kinæk isl**ā**ḥ h**ǣ**zæ æl **takm** |
| When will it be ready? | متى يكون جاهزاً ؟ | mæt**ǣ** yæk**ū**n g**ǣ**hizæn |

# Optician

| | | |
|---|---|---|
| I've broken my glasses. | . كسرت نظارتى [عويناتى] | kasart nazzārati ['owæynāæti] |
| Can you repair them for me? | هل يمكنك اصلاحها ؟ | hæl yomkinæk islāḥæhæ |
| When will they be ready? | متى تكون جاهزة ؟ | mætā tækūn gāhizæ |
| Can you change the lenses? | هل يمكنك تغيير العدسة؟ | hæl yomkinæk tægyīr æl 'ædæsæ |
| I want tinted lenses. | . أريد عدسة غامقة | orīd 'ædæsæ gāmika |
| I want contact lenses. | . أريد عدسات لاصقة | orīd ædæsāt lāsika |
| I'd like to buy a pair of sunglasses. | أريد شراء نظارة شمس. | orīd shirā' nazzārit shæms |
| I'd like to buy a pair of binoculars. | أريد شراء نظارة معظمة. | orīd shirā' nazzara mo'azzima |
| How much do I owe you? | كم الحساب ؟ | kæm æl ḥisāēb |
| Do I pay you now or will you send me your bill? | هل أدفع لك الآن . أم سترسل لى الفاتورة ؟ | hæl ædfæ læk æl'āēn æm sætorsil li æl fatūra |

FOR NUMBERS, see page 175

174

# Reference section

## Where do you come from?

| | | |
|---|---|---|
| Africa | افريقيا | æfrīka |
| Algeria | الجزائر | æl gæzāē'ir |
| Asia | آسيا | 'āēsyāē |
| Australia | استراليا | ostralyā |
| Canada | كندا | kænædæ |
| Egypt | مصر | misr |
| Europe | أوروبا | orobba |
| France | فرنسا | faransa |
| Great Britain | انجلترا | ingiltirā |
| Greece | اليونان | æl yonāēn |
| Ireland | ايرلندا | irlanda |
| Italy | ايطاليا | italyā |
| India | الهند | æl hind |
| Iraq | العراق | æl 'irāk |
| Jordan | الاردن | æl 'ordon |
| Lebanon | لبنان | libnāēn |
| Libya | ليبيا | libyāē |
| Middle East | الشرق الاوسط | æl shark æl 'awsat |
| Morocco | المغرب [مراكش] | æl mægrib [marākish] |
| New Zealand | نيوزيلندا | nyū zilændæ |
| North America | أمريكا الشمالية | æmrīkæ æl shæmāēliyyæ |
| Saudi Arabia | السعودية | æl so'ūdiyyæ |
| South Africa | جنوب افريقيا | gænūb afrikyā |
| South America | أمريكا الجنوبية | æmrīkæ æl gænūbiyyæ |
| Sudan | السودان | æl sūdāēn |
| Syria | سوريا | sūriyyæ |
| Tunisia | تونس | tūnis |
| Turkey | تركيا | torkiyæ |
| USA | الولايات المتحدة | æl wilæyāēt æl mottæḥidæ |
| USSR | روسيا | rosyāē |

# Numbers

| | | | |
|---|---|---|---|
| ٠ | 0 | صفر | sifr |
| ١ | 1 | واحد | wāẹḥid |
| ٢ | 2 | اثنين | 'itnēn |
| ٣ | 3 | ثلاثة | tælāẹtæ |
| ٤ | 4 | أربعة | arbaa |
| ٥ | 5 | خمسة | khæmsæ |
| ٦ | 6 | ستة | sittæ |
| ٧ | 7 | سبعة | sæb'æ |
| ٨ | 8 | ثمانية | tæmāẹnyæ |
| ٩ | 9 | تسعة | tisaa |
| ١٠ | 10 | عشرة | 'ashara |
| ١١ | 11 | أحد عشرة | ḥidāshar |
| ١٢ | 12 | اثنى عشر | itnāshar |
| ١٣ | 13 | ثلاثة عشر | talattāshar |
| ١٤ | 14 | أربعة عشر | arbaatāshar |
| ١٥ | 15 | خمسة عشر | khamastāshar |
| ١٦ | 16 | ستة عشر | sittāshar |
| ١٧ | 17 | سبعة عشر | sabaatāshar |
| ١٨ | 18 | ثمانية عشر | tamantāshar |
| ١٩ | 19 | تسعة عشر | tisaatāshar |
| ٢٠ | 20 | عشرين | 'ishrīn |
| ٢١ | 21 | واحد وعشرين | wāẹḥid wæ 'ishrīn |
| ٢٢ | 22 | اثنين وعشرين | 'itnēn wæ 'ishrīn |
| ٢٣ | 23 | ثلاثة وعشرين | tælāẹtæ wæ 'ishrīn |
| ٢٤ | 24 | أربعة وعشرين | arbaa wa 'ishrīn |
| ٢٥ | 25 | خمسة وعشرين | khæmsæ wæ 'ishrīn |
| ٢٦ | 26 | ستة وعشرين | sittæ wæ 'ishrīn |
| ٢٧ | 27 | سبعة وعشرين | sæb'a wæ 'ishrīn |
| ٢٨ | 28 | ثمانية وعشرين | tæmænyæ wæ 'ishrīn |
| ٢٩ | 29 | تسعة وعشرين | tisaa wæ 'ishrīn |
| ٣٠ | 30 | ثلاثين | tælætin |
| ٣١ | 31 | واحد وثلاثين | wāẹḥid wæ tælætin |

| ٣٢ | 32 | اثنين وثلاثين | 'itnēn wæ tælætīn |
| ٤٠ | 40 | أربعين | ærbi'īn |
| ٥٠ | 50 | خمسين | khæmsīn |
| ٦٠ | 60 | ستين | sittīn |
| ٧٠ | 70 | سبعين | sæb'īn |
| ٨٠ | 80 | ثمانين | tæmænīn |
| ٩٠ | 90 | تسعين | tis'īn |
| ١٠٠ | 100 | مائة | miyyæ |
| ١٠١ | 101 | مائة وواحد | miyyæ wæ wāēhid |
| ١١٠ | 110 | مائة وعشرة | miyyæ wæ ashara |
| ١٢٠ | 120 | مائة وعشرين | miyyæ wæ ishrīn |
| ١٥٠ | 150 | مائة وخمسين | miyyæ wæ khæmsīn |
| ١٦٠ | 160 | مائة وستين | miyyæ wæ sittīn |
| ١٧٠ | 170 | مائة وسبعين | miyyæ wæ sæb'īn |
| ١٨٠ | 180 | مائة وثمانين | miyyæ wæ tæmænīn |
| ١٩٠ | 190 | مائة وتسعين | miyyæ wæ tis'īn |
| ٢٠٠ | 200 | مائتين | mitēn |
| ٣٠٠ | 300 | ثلاثمائة | toltomiyyæ |
| ٤٠٠ | 400 | أربعمائة | rob'omiyyæ |
| ٥٠٠ | 500 | خمسمائة | khomsomiyyæ |
| ٦٠٠ | 600 | ستمائة | sittomiyyæ |
| ٧٠٠ | 700 | سبعمائة | sob'omiyyæ |
| ٨٠٠ | 800 | ثمانمائة | tomnomiyyæ |
| ٩٠٠ | 900 | تسعمائة | tos'omiyyæ |
| ١٠٠٠ | 1,000 | ألف | 'ælf |
| ١١٠٠ | 1,100 | ألف ومائة | 'ælf wæ miyyæ |
| ٥,٠٠٠ | 5,000 | خمسة آلاف | khæmsæt 'ēlāēf |
| ١٠,٠٠٠ | 10,000 | عشرة آلاف | asharat 'ēlāēf |
| ١٠٠,٠٠٠ | 100,000 | مائة ألف | mit 'ælf |
| ١,٠٠٠,٠٠٠ | 1,000,000 | مليون | milyōn |

| | | |
|---|---|---|
| first | أول | ´æwwæl |
| second | ثانى | tǣni |
| third | ثالث | tǣlit |
| fourth | رابع | rābi´ |
| fifth | خامس | khǣmis |
| sixth | سادس | sǣdis |
| seventh | سابع | sǣbi´ |
| eighth | ثامن | tǣmin |
| ninth | تاسع | tǣsi´ |
| tenth | عاشر | ´ǣshir |
| once | مرة | marra |
| twice | مرتين | marritēn |
| three times | ثلاث هرات | tælæt marrāt |
| a half | نصف | noss |
| a quarter | ربع | rob´ |
| one third | ثلث | tilt |
| a pair of | زوج من ... | zōg min |
| a dozen | دستة [دوزينة] | dæstæ [dozzīnæ] |
| 1980 (year) | ١٩٨٠ | ´ælf wæ tos´omiyyæ wæ tæmænin |
| 1981 | ١٩٨١ | ´ælf wæ tos´omiyyæ wǣ-hid wæ tæmænin |
| 1982 | ١٩٨٢ | ´ælf wæ tos´omiyyæ ´itnēn wæ tæmænin |

# Time

الثانية عشرة والربع
(itn**ā**shar wæ rob´)

الواحدة و ثلث
(**w**æḥdæ wæ tilt)

الثانية ونصف الا خمسة
(itn**ē**n wæ noss illæ kh**æ**msæ)

الثالثة والنصف
(tæl**ǣ**tæ wæ noss)

الرابعة ونصف وخمسة
(ar**ba**´a wæ noss wæ kh**æ**msæ)

السادسة الا ثلث
(**sitt**æ illæ tilt)

السابعة الا الربع
(**sæb**´æ illæ rob´)

الثامنة الا عشرة
(tæm**æ**niæ illæ ashara)

التاسعة الا خمسة
(ashara illæ kh**æ**msæ)

العاشرة
(ashara)

العادية عشرة وخمسة
(ḥid**ā**shar wæ kh**æ**msæ)

الثانية عشرة وعشر دقائق
(itn**ā**shar wæ ashara)

# Have you got the time?

| | | |
|---|---|---|
| What time is it? | الساعة كم ؟ | ælsǣæ kǣm |
| It's... | الساعة ... | ælsǣæ |
| Excuse me. Can you tell me the time? | الساعة كم من فضلك ؟ | ælsǣæ kǣm min fadlak |
| I'll meet you tomorrow... | سأقابلك غداً ... | sæ'okābilokæ gædæn |
| at 8 o'clock | الساعة الثامنة | ælsǣæ tæmæmyæ |
| at 2.30 | الساعة الثانية والنصف | ælsǣæ 'itnēn wæ nisf |
| Can I come...? | هل يمكنني الحضور ... ؟ | hæl yomkinoni ælḥodūr |
| I'm sorry I'm late. | آسف على التأخير . | 'āsif 'ælælæl tæ'khīr |
| At what time does... open/close? | متى يفتح / يقفل ... ؟ | mætā yæftæḥ/yakfil |
| What time will it begin/end? | متى يبدأ / ينتهى ؟ | mætā yæbdæ'/yæntæhi |
| At what time should I be there? | متى يجب أن أصل ؟ | mætā yægib æn 'asil |
| At what time will you be there? | متى ستصل ؟ | mætā sætasil |
| after/afterwards | بعد / فيما بعد | bæeæd/fīmā bæeæd |
| before/beforehand | قبل / فيما قبل | kabl/fīmā kabl |
| early | مبكراً | mobækkiran |
| in time | فى الموعد | fil mæw'id |
| late | متأخراً | motæ'ækhkhiran |
| midnight | منتصف الليل | montasaf ællēl |
| noon | الساعة الثانية عشر ظهراً | æl sǣæ 'itnāshar zohran |
| hour | ساعة | sǣæ |
| minute | دقيقة | dakīka |
| second | ثانية [تكة] | sǣnyæ [tækkæ] |
| quarter of an hour | ربع ساعة | rob' sǣæ |
| half an hour | نصف ساعة | nisf sǣæ |

Eastern European Time

Central European Time

Western European Time (G.M.T.)

Atlantic Time

Eastern Time

Central Time

Mountain Time

Pacific Time

Alaska Time

Date Line

Countries which have adopted a time differing from that in the corresponding time zone. Note also that in the USSR, official time is one hour ahead of the time in each corresponding time zone. In summer, numerous countries advance time one hour ahead of standard time.

## Days

| | | |
|---|---|---|
| What day is it today? | أى الايام اليوم ؟ | 'æyyil 'ayyā̆m æl yōm |
| Monday | الاثنين | æl 'itnēn |
| Tuesday | الثلاثاء | æl tælā̆t |
| Wednesday | الاربعاء | æl 'arba' |
| Thursday | الخميس | æl khæmīs |
| Friday | الجمعة | æl gom'æ |
| Saturday | السبت | æl sæbt |
| Sunday | الاحد | æl 'æḥæd |
| in the morning | فى الصباح | fil sabāḥ |
| during the day | خلال اليوم | khilā̆l æl yōm |
| in the afternoon | بعد الظهر | bæædil dohr |
| in the evening | فى المساء | fil mæsā̆' |
| at night | فى الليل | fil lēl |
| yesterday | أمس | 'æms |
| today | اليوم | æl yōm |
| tomorrow | غداً | gædæn |
| two days ago | منذ يومين | min yomēn |
| in three days' time | بعد ثلاثة أيام | bæææd tælæt 'æyyā̆m |
| last week | الاسبوع الماضى | æl 'osbū' æl māḍi |
| next week | الاسبوع القادم | æl 'osbū' æl kādim |
| birthday | عيد ميلاد | 'id milā̆d |
| day | يوم | yōm |
| day off | يوم أجازة [فرصة] | yōm 'ægā̆zæ [firsa] |
| holidays | الاجازة [الفرصة] | æl 'ægā̆zæ [æl firsa] |
| month | شهر | shahr |
| vacation | أجازة [فرصة] | 'ægā̆zæ [firsa] |
| week | أسبوع | 'osbū' |
| weekday | يوم فى وسط الاسبوع | yōm fi wistil 'osbū' |
| weekend | عطلة آخر الاسبوع | 'otlit 'ā̆khir æl 'osbū' |
| working day | يوم عمل | yōm 'æmæl |

## Months

| | | |
|---|---|---|
| January | ينايـر [كانون الثانى] | yænāæyir [kānūn æltāæni] |
| February | فبرايـر [شباط] | fibrāyir [shbāt] |
| March | مـارس [آذار] | māæris ['āzār] |
| April | أبريـل [نيسـان] | æbrīl [nisāæn] |
| May | مايو [آيـار] | māæyo ['āyār] |
| June | يـونيو [حزيران] | yonyo [ḥozæyrān] |
| July | يـوليو [تموز] | yolyo [tæmmūz] |
| August | أغسطس [آب] | 'agostos ['āæb] |
| September | سـبتمبر [أيلـول] | sibtæmbir ['æylūl] |
| October | اكتـوبر [تشرين الاول] | oktōbar [tishrin æl 'æwwæl] |
| November | نوفمبر [تشرين الثانى] | nōvæmbir [tishrin æl tāæni] |
| December | ديسمبر [كانون الاول] | disæmbir [kāænūn æl 'æwwæl] |
| since June | منذ شهر يونيو [حزيران] | monzo shahr yonyo [ḥozæyrān] |
| during the month of August | خلال شهر أغسطس [آب] | khilāæl shahr 'agostos ['āæb] |
| last month | الشهر الماضى | æl shahr æl māædi |
| next month | الشهر القادم | æl shahr æl kāædim |
| July 1 | أول يوليو | 'æwwæl yolyo [tæmmūz] |
| March 17 | السابع عشر من مارس [آذار] | æl sāæbii 'ashar min māæris ['āzār] |

## Seasons

| | | |
|---|---|---|
| spring | الربيع | æl rabīi |
| summer | الصيف | æl sēf |
| autumn | الغريف | æl khærif |
| winter | الشتاء | æl shitāæ' |
| in spring | فى الربيع | fil rabīi |
| during the summer | خلال الصيف | khilāæl æl sēf |
| in autumn | فى الغريف | fil kærif |
| during the winter | خلال الشتاء | khilāæl æl shitāæ' |

## Public holidays

Two kinds of calendars are in use in Arab countries. The Gregorian calendar—which is the one we use—is current in normal daily activities. However, newspapers, official documents and certain public holidays follow the Islamic lunar calendar which begins with the Hegira, or emigration of the Prophet Mohammed from Mecca to Medina. 1980 A.D. is the year 1400 of this calendar. The lunar year has twelve months of 29 or 30 days, and thus is approximately 10 days shorter than the Gregorian or solar year.

The names of the Hegira months are:

| | |
|---|---|
| محرم | moharram |
| صفر | safar |
| ربيع الاول | rabīi æl 'æwwæl |
| ربيع الثانى | rabīi æl tǣni |
| جمادى الاولى | gæmǣdæ æl 'ūlǣ |
| جمادى الثانية | gæmǣdæ æl tænyæ |
| رجب | rægæb |
| شعبان | shææbǣn |
| رمضان | ramadān |
| شوال | shæwwǣl |
| ذو القعدة | zul kiida |
| ذو الحجة | zul higgæ |

Given below are the most important Moslem holidays.

| | |
|---|---|
| 1st moharram | Hegira or Muslim New Year's Day |
| 12th rabīi æl 'æwwæl | Birth of the Prophet Mohammed |
| 1st to 3th shæwwæl | Ramadan Baïram ('id æl fitr) celebrating the end of the holy month of Ramadan which is marked by month-long fasting from sunrise to sunset. |
| 9th to 13th zul higgæ | Kurban Baïram ('id æl 'adha) celebrating God's mercy toward Abraham in sparing his son; this is the period during which Muslims make a pilgrimage to Mecca. |

While there may be additional regional holidays, only national holidays in Egypt (E), Jordan (J) or Lebanon (L) are cited below:

| | | | | |
|---|---|---|---|---|
| January 1 | New Year's Day (Gregorian) | | J | L |
| January 15 | Arbor Day | | J | |
| March 8 | Syrian Revolution Day | E | | |
| March 22 | Founding of the Arab League | | J | L |
| May 1 | Labour Day | E | J | L |
| May 6 | Martyr's Day | | | L |
| May 25 | Independence Day | | J | |
| June 18 | Evacuation Day | E | | |
| July 23 | Revolution Anniversary | E | | |
| August 11 | Accession Day (King Hussein) | | J | |
| August 15 | Assumption Day | | | L |
| September 1 | Libyan Revolution Day | E | | |
| October 6 | October War Day | E | | |
| November 1 | All Saints' Day | | | L |
| November 14 | King Hussein's Birthday | | J | |
| November 22 | Independence Day | | | L |
| December 23 | Victory Day | E | | |
| December 25 | Christmas Day | | J | L |
| December 31 | Foreign Troops Evacuation Day | | | L |

| | | | | |
|---|---|---|---|---|
| Movable dates: | Good Friday (Catholic or Orthodox) | | J | L |
| | Easter Monday (Catholic or Orthodox) | | J | L |
| | Spring Day, first Monday after Easter | E | | |

## The year-round temperatures

| | Amman | Cairo | Beirut |
|---|---|---|---|
| January | 39–54 °F | 47–65 °F | 51–62 °F |
| February | 40–56 | 48–69 | 51–63 |
| March | 43–60 | 52–75 | 54–66 |
| April | 49–73 | 51–83 | 58–72 |
| May | 57–83 | 63–91 | 64–78 |
| June | 61–87 | 68–95 | 69–83 |
| July | 65–89 | 70–96 | 73–87 |
| August | 65–90 | 71–95 | 74–89 |
| September | 62–88 | 68–90 | 73–86 |
| October | 57–81 | 65–86 | 69–81 |
| November | 50–70 | 58–78 | 61–73 |
| December | 42–59 | 50–68 | 55–65 |

## Conversion tables

To change centimetres into inches, multiply by .39.

To change inches into centimetres, multiply by 2.54.

## Centimetres and inches

|        | in.   | feet  | yards |
|--------|-------|-------|-------|
| 1 mm   | 0.039 | 0.003 | 0.001 |
| 1 cm   | 0.39  | 0.03  | 0.01  |
| 1 dm   | 3.94  | 0.32  | 0.10  |
| 1 m    | 39.40 | 3.28  | 1.09  |

|        | mm    | cm    | m     |
|--------|-------|-------|-------|
| 1 in.  | 25.4  | 2.54  | 0.025 |
| 1 ft.  | 304.8 | 30.48 | 0.305 |
| 1 yd.  | 914.4 | 91.44 | 0.914 |

(32 metres = 35 yards)

## Temperature

To convert Centigrade into degrees Fahrenheit, multiply Centigrade by 1.8 and add 32.

To convert degrees Fahrenheit into Centigrade, subtract 32 from Fahrenheit and divide by 1.8.

## Metres and feet

The figure in the middle stands for both metres and feet, e.g ,
1 metre = 3.281 ft. and 1 foot = 0.30 m.

| Metres | | Feet |
|---|---|---|
| 0.30 | 1 | 3.281 |
| 0.61 | 2 | 6.563 |
| 0.91 | 3 | 9.843 |
| 1.22 | 4 | 13.124 |
| 1.52 | 5 | 16.403 |
| 1.83 | 6 | 19.686 |
| 2.13 | 7 | 22.967 |
| 2.44 | 8 | 26.248 |
| 2.74 | 9 | 29.529 |
| 3.05 | 10 | 32.810 |
| 3.35 | 11 | 36.091 |
| 3.66 | 12 | 39.372 |
| 3.96 | 13 | 42.635 |
| 4.27 | 14 | 45.934 |
| 4.57 | 15 | 49.215 |
| 4.88 | 16 | 52.496 |
| 5.18 | 17 | 55.777 |
| 5.49 | 18 | 59.058 |
| 5.79 | 19 | 62.339 |
| 6.10 | 20 | 65.620 |
| 7.62 | 25 | 82.023 |
| 15.24 | 50 | 164.046 |
| 22.86 | 75 | 246.069 |
| 30.48 | 100 | 328.092 |

## Other conversion charts

## Weight conversion

The figure in the middle stands for both kilograms and pounds,
e.g., 1 kilogram = 2.205 1b. and 1 pound = 0.45 kilograms.

| Kilograms (kg.) | | Avoirdupois pounds |
|---|---|---|
| 0.45 | 1 | 2.205 |
| 0.91 | 2 | 4.409 |
| 1.36 | 3 | 6.614 |
| 1.81 | 4 | 8.818 |
| 2.27 | 5 | 11.023 |
| 2.72 | 6 | 13.227 |
| 3.17 | 7 | 15.432 |
| 3.62 | 8 | 17.636 |
| 4.08 | 9 | 19.841 |
| 4.53 | 10 | 22.045 |
| 6.80 | 15 | 33.068 |
| 9.06 | 20 | 44.089 |
| 11.33 | 25 | 55.113 |
| 22.65 | 50 | 110.225 |
| 34.02 | 75 | 165.338 |
| 45.30 | 100 | 220.450 |

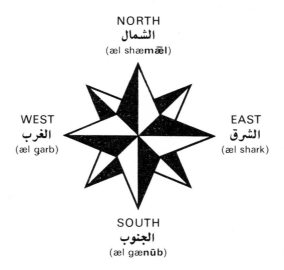

NORTH
الشمال
(æl shæmāēl)

WEST
الغرب
(æl garb)

EAST
الشرق
(æl shark)

SOUTH
الجنوب
(æl gænūb)

# What does that sign mean?

| | |
|---|---|
| احترس | Caution |
| احترس من الكلب | Beware of the dog |
| ادفع | Push |
| استعلامات | Information |
| اسحب | Pull |
| خاص | Private |
| خالى [فاضى] | Vacant |
| خروج | Exit |
| الخزينة | Cashier |
| خطر | Danger |
| خطر الموت | Mortal danger |
| دخول | Entrance |
| الدخول مجاناً | Free entrance |
| دق الجرس من فضلك | Please ring |
| رجال | Gentlemen |
| سيدات | Ladies |
| طريق خاص | Private road |
| للايجار | For hire (rent) |
| للبيع | For sale |
| مباع | Sold out |
| مشغول | Occupied |
| مصعد | Lift (Elevator) |
| مغلق | Closed |
| ... ممنوع | ...forbidden |
| ممنوع التصوير | No photographs |
| ممنوع التدخين | No smoking |
| ممنوع الدخول | No entrance |
| ممنوع اللمس | Don't touch |
| ممنوع المرور | No trespassing |
| منطقة عسكرية | Military area |

# Emergency!

By the time the emergency is upon you, it's too late to turn to this page to find the Arabic for "I'll scream if you...". So have a look at this list beforehand—and, if you want to be on the safe side, learn the expressions shown in capitals.

| Call the police | اطلب البوليس | 'otlob æl bolīs |
| CAREFUL | انتبه | 'intæbih |
| Come here | تعالى هنا | tæǣlæ honǣ |
| Come in | ادخل | 'odkhol |
| Danger | خطر | khatar |
| Fire | حريق | ḥærik |
| Gas | غاز | gǣz |
| Get a doctor | اطلب دكتور | 'otlob doktōr |
| Get help quickly | اطلب المساعدة بسرعة | 'otlob ælmosǣ'ædæ bisoraa |
| Go away | انصرف | 'insarif |
| HELP | النجدة | ælnægdæ |
| I'm ill | أنا مريض | ænǣ marid |
| I'm lost | أنا تهت | ænǣ toht |
| Keep your hands to yourself | ابعد يدك | 'ibiid yædæk |
| Leave me alone | اتركنى لحالى | 'itrokni liḥǣli |
| Lie down | ارقد | 'orkod |
| Listen | استمع | istæmii |
| Look | انظر | onzor |
| LOOK OUT | احترس | iḥtæris |
| POLICE | بوليس [شرطة] | bōlīs [shorta] |
| Quick | بسرعة | bisoraa |
| STOP | قف | kiff |
| Stop here | قف هنا | kiff honǣ |
| Stop that man | امسك هذا الرجل | 'æmsik hǣzæ æl ragol |
| STOP THIEF | امسك حرامى | 'æmsik ḥarāmi |
| Stop or I'll scream | قف والا سأصرخ | kif wæ 'illǣ sæ'asrokh |

FOR CAR ACCIDENTS, see page 149

# Index

192

## Quick reference page

| | | |
|---|---|---|
| Please / Excuse me. | . من فضلك | min **fad**lak |
| Thank you. | . شكراً | **shok**ran |
| Yes / No. | . أيوة / لا | ʾ**æy**wæ/lǣ |
| I beg your pardon / I'm sorry. | . آسف | ʾǣsif |
| Waiter, please. | . من فضلك | min **fad**lak |
| How much is that? | بكم هذا ؟ | bikæm **hǣ**zæ |
| Where are the toilets? | أين التواليت ؟ | ʾ**æy**næl twæ**lit** |

| تواليت (twæ**lit**) | Toilets |
|---|---|
| رجال<br>(rig**ǣl**) | سيدات<br>(sæyyi**dǣt**) |

| | | |
|---|---|---|
| Help me, please. | . ساعدنى من فضلك | sæʾ**id**ni min **fad**lak |
| What time is it? | الساعة كم ؟ | æls**ǣ**æ kǣm |
| Where's the ... consulate? | ... اين القنصلية | ʾ**æy**næ sel konso**liy**yæ |
| American<br>English | الامريكية<br>الانجليزية | sel'æmri**kiy**yæ<br>sel'ingili**siy**yæ |
| What does this mean?<br>I don't understand. | ما معنى هذا ؟<br>. لا أفهم | mǣ **mæ**ænǣ **hǣ**zæ<br>lǣ ʾ**æf**hæm |
| Just a minute. I'll point out the word. | . لعظة . سأشير الى الكلمة | **lah**za. sæʾ**osh**ir ʾ**il**æl **kil**mæ |
| Do you speak English? | هل تتكلم انجليزى ؟ | hæl tætæ**kæl**læm ingi**li**zi |